Behind those Heels

Behind those *Heels*

Ten Powerful Messages
to Inspire and Ignite Change

Cassie Ferrer and Debbie Belnavis-Brimble
with Eight Other Amazing Women

Published by Carnelian Moon Publishing

www.carnelianmoonpublishing.com

Copyright © 2020 Behind those Heels, behindthoseheels.com.

All rights reserved. No part of this book may be reproduced, distributed, or transmitted in any form or by any means, electronic or mechanical, including photocopying and recording, or by any information storage and retrieval system, without express permission in writing from the author or publisher. The only exception is by a reviewer, who may quote short excerpts in a review.

Cover Design by Jennifer Insignares
Editing by Althea Gray
Interior Layout Design by Simon Brimble

Printed Book ISBN: 978-1-7360470-0-2
eBook ISBN: 978-1-7360470-1-9

Dedication

We dedicate this book to all the women around the globe who have overcome or are currently overcoming major challenges. The goal is to inspire others to share their stories and create a movement allowing women to share their truth, being their full authentic selves. Using your authentic voice and freeing yourself from judgement of self or others.

We also dedicate this book to all the women who are already being huge role models in their own right, who have said yes to sharing their stories with you and being fully transparent for your transformation.

To the loved ones who have stood by us as we live our dreams daily, Diego, Simon, Camila, Jaiden and Chase. We love you and do this for you!

Acknowledgement

There are so many that we would like to acknowledge and thank for their unwavering support and love, for the Founders of the *Behind those Heels* movement, Cassie Ferrer and Debbie Belnavis-Brimble. First and foremost, our families who have supported us and provided assistance during lots of late nights, looking after the children while meetings took place. Thank you to our husbands, Diego Ferrer and Simon Brimble. Secondly, we would like to thank our children who have motivated us and give us our greatest reason for being on this mission to support others in being the best version of themselves, Camila, Jaiden and Chase. Your Moms are doing this for you!

We would like to thank our parents for giving us their best versions of themselves and guiding us to do our best and be our best always. We would also like to thank all of our coaches and mentors who have guided, encouraged and cheered us along our journey, there are too many of you to mention.

We wouldn't have this book without all the ladies who believed in the *Behind those Heels* mission, who shared their stories with us on the *Behind those Heels Podcast* and here in our very first book. Thank you for being here with us. We are filled with so much gratitude for you and appreciate you and the journey you have been on yourself. You are extraordinary, and together we are spreading even more hope in our world.

To our publishers, Carnelian Moon Publishing who have been very generous in guiding us through the process of publishing our very first book and making the journey a blissful one. Finding us the Editor, Graphics Design for our book cover and our Interior Layout Designer. We appreciate your dedicated work and commitment to our mission.

Finally, without Cassie's vision, Behind those Heels would not exist and without Debbie's expertise, this book would not have been created yet, so huge thanks for our joint vision, our beautiful partnership and all the future successes to come. It takes courage to come together and share our journey so transparently. We are grateful for each other. Watch this space for more about *Behind those Heels*.

With so much gratitude.

Contents

Introduction	1
The Bottom was a Moment Away	
by Adele Mason	4
It All Happened For Me	
by Cassie Ferrer	13
The Girl Who Stopped Laughing	
by Ruth Murray	24
The Lies that Caged Me	
by Georgia Pomrenke	33
Mindset, Magic, and Manifestation	
by Michelle Montero	42
Living and Thriving with Depression	
by Debbie Brady	52
Becoming Me	
by Tania Hunter-Gilligan	60
Find your voice	
by Sara Olson	70
Finding My Brilliance through Forgiveness	
by Debbie Belnavis-Brimble	76
Releasing the Control of Food and My Secret Shames	
by Jennifer Hernandez	87
Your Message Inspires the World	100
About Behind those Heels	102
About Our Authors	104

Introduction

Welcome to the *Behind those Heels* movement where her message inspires the world. *Behind those Heels* is the vision of Cassie Ferrer, Award Winning Financial Leader. Cassie met a group of well-dressed, accomplished, and confident women through her volunteer network, who shared unexpected stories of how they overcame their extraordinary challenges and found fulfillment in their lives. She was instantly inspired by their uplifting stories. One of the things she noticed as they all spoke about their individual journeys was that they all wore the most exquisite shoes which were all high heels. She thought to herself, *'how cool would it be to come up with a book to share the stories of women like these and what if that book was called Behind those Heels?'*

This thought stayed with her for years until Cassie attended a personal development seminar in 2012 that changed her life forever. Although she was experiencing major success in her corporate career, as a First Vice President and managing an underwriting team handling loan portfolio sizes of over $50 million dollars, Cassie realized that she wasn't living her purpose or being fulfilled. During the seminar, she remembered her thought about the *Behind those Heels* book many years before, and it reignited something inside of her so strong. Cassie made it her personal goal that day to start an organization called *Behind those Heels* to share the stories similar to the ones she already heard and there would be a book with the same name.

Cassie joined forces with Debbie Belnavis-Brimble, Inner Brilliance Coach and Mentor, #1 International Best-Selling Author and Publisher at Carnelian Moon Publishing to form *Behind those Heels*. The vision quickly grew into a movement where multiple platforms would be made available to share the stories of women around the world, a podcast, books, events and support for women. Cassie and Debbie both know how empowering and inspiring it is for others when stories are shared and people become transparent and share their truth.

In February 2020 they launched the **Behind those Heels Movement** where women share their powerful stories using various platforms including our *Behind those Heels* podcast, books and events, encouraging others to take action and seek support to enhance their lives.

This book has been a labor of love for all the authors involved. We have all poured our hearts and souls in being fully transparent and sharing our journey and transformation to support you in your healing journey. We have shared our stories of homelessness, abandonment, failed relationship, domestic violence, grief, weight challenges, forgiveness and so much more. We have shared our stories for you to know that you are never alone, you can claim your success, you too have the inner power to embrace the positive changes that your heart desires. We have shared some of our strategies to support your own personal growth. As you read each story, know that you also have a story inside of you and your story can also inspire others to fully embrace their authenticity, inner power, self-love, self-worth and confidence. We believe that everyone has a *Behind those Heels* story to share, have you shared yours yet?

Enjoy your journey with us!

Listen to even more stories on our *Behind those Heels Podcast* on your favorite podcast player or from our website at www.behindthoseheels.com/podcast.

The Bottom was a Moment Away

by Adele Mason

Winter, 2014, I am training for my first half marathon. I was eating well, I often have two glasses of wine as an indulgence with dinner. I prefer very dry white, always pouring it in hand painted glasses that were a wedding gift.

Winter, 2018, my marriage has ended without warning. I leave my matrimonial home, the city and life I have known, with my life in garbage bags. Along with white wine, vodka and gin, I am now regularly drinking mouthwash.

My story begins long before this, when I was born into a good home, to parents who wanted me very much. We were a happy trio until the joyful day my brother arrived eight years later, making us a family of four. On the same day my father began his new job as a high school principal.

My parents were deeply loving, totally devoted, and very strict.

I bridled against their strictness even in my earliest memories, which are fraught with conflicting recollections of childhood happiness, frustrations at feeling controlled, and (though I couldn't have articulated it then) significant depression. Despite the stability of my home environment and the dedication of both parents, I always felt as though the bottom was a moment away from falling out of my world—eventually, it did.

I was always mercurial in temperament, hot-blooded, hot-headed, creative and defiant down to my bones. I bridled at restrictions and relished the opportunity to prove that I didn't need to abide by them. I thrilled at the rebellion of historical bad boys like Lord Byron and F. Scott Fitzgerald, relating to their badassery, their debauchery, and their genius. I wanted to be like them, and by the end of my drinking days, I was far more like them than I ever bargained for.

In 2001, I began dating the man who would become my husband. We should have had the good sense to know we weren't right for each other. Yet, a mutual respect, shared laughter, and the blindness of youth led us all the way down the altar.

A mere five months after we were married, I dove without warning into the bottom of a bottle of whiskey. At the time, I was working for an insurance company, putting in astronomically long hours of overtime. I was also dealing with a third bout of significant depression and was despondent at having to once again be back on medication. I needed a break from being myself for a minute, and alcohol was just the thing.

For some people, drinking alcohol creeps up on them. For me, I went from being a non-drinker to an alcoholic immediately. I rarely, and only with great effort, could have a polite drink or three and then stop. Usually, it was an out-of-control binge.

I thought for a time that whiskey was the problem, and in fact, there always was something different and darker about the way I responded to whiskey. But the problem wasn't what was in the bottle. The problem was ME. The problem was *alcoholism*.

On May 3, 2005, the spring before I started graduate school, I drank a mickey of whiskey, (almost a pint) in less than 90 minutes. I passed out on my back, and if not for my dog, would have sunk into unconsciousness. As it was, her barking kept me out of the depths so that when I realized I needed to vomit, I turned over on my stomach and proceeded to spew whiskey and undigested food all over the living room carpet.

I switched to vodka coolers, which worked for a while, until, of course, it didn't.

On November 23, 2007, I was bent over our downstairs toilet, vomiting out red wine. I hated red wine, but I was long past caring what anything tasted like. My husband was standing in the doorway, arms crossed. Through the waves of nausea, I heard him saying that this was about to affect his career in a major way, and I needed to stop.

He was a university professor, and was preparing to go forward for tenure, and needed the coming months to prove himself as a scholar. So, my drunken shenanigans were wearing him out and affecting the quality of his work and his energy and concentration.

Right up until that moment, I had gotten away with my drinking. But suddenly, it was about to cost us everything.

I left my PhD program and stopped drinking out of fear for my husband's job and our future as a married couple. In an act of poetry from the universe, our daughter came along a year to the day later, on November 23, 2008. For almost two and a half years I didn't consume any alcohol, not a single drop.

I missed it, of course, at times. But early motherhood had my full attention. I got on with life and would go days at a time thinking only of baby bottles, not wine bottles. It seemed like my drinking days were truly a thing of the past.

Then, in the winter of 2010, in a cognitive error typical of the thinking disease that is alcoholism, I decided I was healed enough to start drinking again. I figured I had learned my lesson.

I started to drink cautiously and I would go on to drink reasonably, responsibly, and without consequence for more than four years.

The half marathon in May of 2014 was a high point of my adult life. I had been wanting to run *that* race, on *that* course, since my father ran the full marathon twenty-nine years earlier, when I was only six years old.

I still remember taking the first few steps across the starting line. There is a moment in the movie *Deep Blue Sea* where the character Dr. Susan McCallister says *"You wait your whole life for a single moment, and then one day it's tomorrow"*, and I understood that sentiment exactly. For 29 years, I had been wanting to run on those streets, in my hometown. For months, I had trained through brutal cold, biting wind. I had lost a toenail. Strained the iliotibial (IT) band on my right leg. Lost fifteen pounds. Adjusted my social life to accommodate my training schedule. And there it was, laid out in front of me - the race, mine to run. The finish line, mine to cross, a mere 21.1 kilometers standing between me and a finisher's medal around my neck.

It was the moment of a lifetime to cross that line, stagger towards my waiting family and sink down onto the pavement into an exhausted, sobbing heap. Mission accomplished; dream come true.

But then it was over. The rigorous training regimen which had kept my demons at bay was gone. And alcohol came back into my life with a vengeance, when pneumonia, the end of a treasured friendship, and terrifying health scare with my father wore down my defenses.

By the middle of 2016, I was regularly drinking mouthwash. In desperation, I voluntarily checked myself into detox and then rehab that July. However, a mere month in rehab is nothing, nowhere close to enough time to wrestle down the behemoth that is addiction, and I was drinking again before my brother's wedding in mid-October.

I returned to school in late December of 2016 for training in a career as a medical office administrator. That would stop my drinking, I thought. An academic "hobby". On February 17, 2017, while celebrating the good grades, my husband announced that our marriage was over. We hadn't been happy for some time, but the news was a terrible shock.

Eleven days later, I left the house, the home and the city I had known for eight years, with my life in garbage bags and my daughter at my side, as my father drove us back to the house where I grew up.

In those eleven days, family services had already become involved. I was experiencing very dark thoughts, and sought help at a provincial hospital widely renowned for its specialized mental health care. A social worker there falsely recorded that I had overdosed on pills with my young child in the home. On the basis of this, she notified family services.

Addicted mothers are caught in a terrible trap: Don't seek help, and someone is likely to report you. Seek help, and you are likely to be reported, anyway. In essence, the system sends this message: If you are a mother, for the love of God, don't struggle with addiction. You might lose your children, and if you do, you might never get them back.

Back in my parents' home, I felt grateful to be back in my hometown, and yet enraged at the humiliation of going from the mistress of a spacious four-bedroom house to being crammed into a room so small I banged my hip every morning until the day I moved out when I made the bed.

My parents tried to help. They put their lives aside, cleared their social calendars, stepped in to parent both my daughter and I. They were patient and accessible and plugged in. They were generous with their time, their energy, their grocery bill, and the space in their house at a stage of life when it should have belonged only to them.

My parents had been married for more than forty years. They couldn't understand the trauma of a marriage breakup. Of the one being broken up with. Neither could they understand that you don't stop an alcoholic by refusing to give her the keys to your car. Someone with a substance use disorder will find a way, and I did, always.

As my drinking worsened, so did the tensions between us. Addiction is a family disease, and our family was breaking under the weight of it. On Father's Day, 2018, I got so drunk that I lunged at my father. I either punched him or pushed him---I was too drunk to remember. I do remember the look on his face right before he tackled me, and my mother pulling him off me. It was a hopeless tangle, of people and pain, of problems, of pathology. We were all almost beyond saving.

On the night of July 18, 2018, I was drunk yet again. Drinking away my time in a day hospital program during which we were, of course, not supposed to be using any substances of any kind. I was in the middle of a routine I had practiced a thousand times before: Get drunk at home. Take a cab to a restaurant near my on-again, off-again partner's home. Get drunker. Then finish out the evening with him, where we would either fight, or have sex, or both.

On this night though, I made a decision I had never made before, but which I have often thought of since as divine grace: I let my mother drive me. When my partner refused to answer his buzzer, I went to a nearby bar. I am told I kept telling my mother to call an ambulance because I wasn't handling this well. I recall throwing things, but what I was throwing or why, I don't remember.

Abruptly, I took off into the night, leaving everything behind, including my shoes. I remember the hot, sharp pavement against my feet. The rage when he wouldn't answer. The helplessness, the danger, the absolute *knowing* that no one would hear me and no one would come.

I also remember knowing that *rock bottom was finally here*.

Past the point of reason or thought, though, I took off on foot once again, down the long driveway, drunk enough to be stupid, not drunk enough to be relieved of my desire for more alcohol. When four police cars surrounded me, and a young male officer got out and spoke to me softly, I was still *fighting*--life, myself, everything.

All of a sudden, I was done. I raised my hands over my head, asked for help, and climbed, barefoot, into the back of the cruiser.

In the beginning, sobriety was sweatpants, planning my day out by the hour, and falling into bed at 2 p.m, exhausted from the effort of being awake, and being myself, without alcohol.

For a time, my addictive tendencies would go out sideways, as gambling, dating, and eating took the place of drinking. It is only in hindsight that I realize how truly and profoundly sick I was, how damaged my brain had become. In order to survive being sober from alcohol, for a while I had to become addicted to other things. My brain had become that dependent, that disordered.

I would cry, for hours and sometimes days at a time. Torrents of tears, oceans of pain, a lifetime of hidden trauma and a thousand unprocessed griefs that had led me down into the bottom of a bottle. When all was said and done, I cried for almost 22 months before steadying out.

Sobriety isn't always easy. It isn't always fun. But the sharp edges of the early weeks have smoothed into some measure of peace. I no longer engage in any addictive patterns. That need has receded, like a shadow. I think I will always be a little bit haunted by the ghost of its memory, its damage.

Trauma therapy, occupational therapy, peer support, my parents' unyielding commitment to their tempestuous firstborn, and a second chance at love have been essential parts of my ongoing healing. It's a journey that will never end.

My glass is empty. But one day at a time, my cup runneth over anyway.

Adele Mason
WomenShift Coaching, Inc.
Canada
womenshiftcoaching.com

It All Happened For Me

by Cassie Ferrer

I was only 17 years old feeling confused, sitting on a plane with tears rolling down my face, not knowing where I would end up.

My life changed completely the moment I stepped onto that plane. As the plane took off, I was crying uncontrollably. I couldn't help but wonder why things kept happening to me.

Throughout the journey, so many thoughts were going through my mind. Who will be picking me up at the airport? Would they know who I am?

Throughout my life, I chose the role of the perfect victim, waiting for someone or something to rescue me. I felt completely hopeless and out of control. I would have never expected that later I would create an organization that can impact millions of women and starting an incredible movement.

My life story began when I was born in Hong Kong to my mom, who was a teenager.

My parents met when they were working part time at a fast-food restaurant. My father moved to the U.S shortly after they met. When he returned to Hong Kong to visit my mom, she ended up getting pregnant with me. My father would visit me and my mother a few times when he could and they eventually got married after I was born. When I was around two years old, my father divorced my mom as he decided to get remarried to my stepmother in the U.S. and all visitations stopped.

My mom raised me by herself as a single mother. It was us against the world and my mom did the very best she could. She worked several jobs to make ends meet while providing for me. When I was little, my mom would take me to get my favorite street food, Shui Mai, similar to dim sum from a Chinese restaurant, before starting her work. I would be enjoying my food while watching her work.

Even as a little girl, I remembered being impressed watching her work as she was so quick on a calculator. I was shocked how quickly her fingers moved and I was fascinated when the paper came out with numbers printed on it. It's funny that I ended up working in the financial sector with numbers and my fingers would move just as fast when I was keying in data. I wonder if I got this natural talent from my mom.

Even though we did not have a lot, being with my mom was the best thing in my life. My mom and I were very close when I was little and I was always artistic as a kid and used to draw pictures for my mom. I would give her a sweet note with "I love you" with my drawings as she dropped me off at the babysitter.

It was probably the most difficult time in my mom's life, being a single parent with multiple jobs. I treasured every minute of the time we spent together.

I remembered she talked about how hurt she was when she received the letter from my dad informing her that he was getting married. She knew then the visitations would stop. When I was a toddler, I would write short notes and letters to my father and asked my mom to send them. One time, my mom told me that she would not send them and that my father had *abandoned us*. I felt that it was my fault that he left us. This is where my insecurities started to develop from my childhood. Growing up, I couldn't understand why my father would leave me and not want to stay connected.

When I was about five or six years old, my mom met and married my stepdad. Their marriage started very rocky because my stepdad came from a traditional Chinese family. His family found it difficult because my mother had a daughter before they were married. I remembered having to use a different last name when I attended my stepdad's family gathering so his family's friends would not question me for being the stepchild. This created so much confusion for me because I was so young and yet I had to lie about my identity.

Despite these challenges, I was grateful that I got to move in with my mom and my stepdad instead of living with my babysitter. My mom then got pregnant with my brother when I was seven and became a stay at home mom for a while. It was probably the best memory I had as we got to go to the park after school and got to spend time together as a family.

When my brother became a toddler, my mom returned to

work. Hong Kong is a very fast paced environment and full-time employees often have long working hours. With both of my parents working long hours, my mom and my stepdad started having communication issues, no doubt because they were not seeing each other often enough. This created stress for my stepdad and with the negative influence from friends, my stepfather started developing a gambling problem.

This started to create a negative impact on our family as we often had to move from one apartment to the next as our rent payments were becoming late.

My mom became a realtor at one point and had the opportunity to purchase our first home. She was always an excellent salesperson and she exceled at her realtor career. We had a nice home in a safe area. My brother and I enjoyed the extra space. My mom was overjoyed that my brother and I had our own room.

One day, my mom found out that we were late on our mortgage as the scheduled payments were not made. My stepdad also had some credit card debts from gambling. The house ended up being foreclosed and my parents ended up separating for a while. With the help of a marriage counselor, my parents got back together and their communication improved, along with their marriage, even if my stepdad's gambling problem didn't stop completely.

My mom always wanted me to excel in everything I did and to be the best at school. She was always very tough on me and had high expectations. I hated to disappoint my mom because I knew how hard she had to work to take care of me all alone for so many years. I remember how mad she was when I received a

B on my English paper.

While I was excelling at school, I did not have many friends. I was advised by some teachers that I was being self-centered. I did not know what it meant back then, but I realized that it was due to my insecurity from my early childhood, and abandonment. This led me to always wanting to gain the attention of others, hoping that I would start to feel wanted, which made others think I wanted everything to be about me. Of course, my behavior did not make me popular at school. I was often being isolated by the other girls and didn't make many friends.

When I became a teenager, I started being very rebellious. I was so desperate to be accepted by a remotely popular group I started to make major mistakes. I was dating older boys, trying cigarettes, drinking alcohol, and being in night clubs instead of going to classes. I then moved out to live with my boyfriend at the time and his family when I was 15. I no longer felt like I fit in with my own family, I was only the stepdaughter to my stepdad. I felt that he favored my brother when I was living with them.

My mom saw me headed down the wrong path and as always wanted the best for me. She could see what could be the worst that could happen if she did nothing. Feeling desperate, my mom made the best decision at the time. She decided that I should move to the U.S. and attend college. She contacted my father and let him know that I was moving to the U.S. She asked him to help look after me when I attended college.

When my mother told me that I was moving to the U.S. I was thinking that she was simply sending me away to get rid of her problem. All my feelings of insecurity came flooding back as I remembered how I felt when my father had left me all those years before. At that time, I had developed some close friendships and it was difficult for me to leave them and leave everything I knew. I was not prepared to move to a foreign place living with people I barely knew.

Getting on the plane for the first time, I felt nervous and sad. After over twenty hours, I arrived in Seattle. It was gloomy when I got off the plane. My father was expecting me and he was excited to meet me. I was seventeen at the time when I first met him again. Obviously, I didn't even recognize him when I saw him at the airport. I met his wife and his children for the first time. While his family seemed welcoming, I almost felt a bit jealous and angry at the same time. I was thinking that because of this family, he left my mom and I in Hong Kong.

However, I enjoyed spending time and getting to know my half brothers and sisters and my stepmother. I didn't get along with my father, because I found him to be very stubborn in his ways. The adjustment was at times challenging, as it was with his family while living in his house. My English wasn't very good as I had just arrived from Hong Kong, so the issues could have been as a result of miscommunications or the cultural difference. I decided to move out shortly after a few months with a roommate and started college. I did see my father and his family during the holidays, and our relationship has improved over the years.

My journey during college was not easy. Even though I learned written English at school, my spoken English was weak. Having to learn another language while trying to make friends was a major adjustment. I also had to work multiple jobs while attending college to help pay for my expenses. At times, it got very tough as I was simply tired from working while having to complete homework assignments.

I was very fortunate. I met many mentors and friends along the way who helped me tremendously while attending college. I had some teachers that knew my struggles and encouraged me to do my best. They suggested that I take on fewer classes and not to get too overwhelmed. They also allowed me to see the opportunities that could be provided to me once I graduate college. I also met some friends who were very understanding and provided me with great support. They helped me feel better being in a place I did not quite understand at that time.

After five long years of perseverance and hard work, I graduated from college with a BA in Finance and Marketing with high honor then went on and received my MBA. I felt so proud receiving my degree. I have thought about giving up feeling exhausted from having to work and doing school work afterward and often had to stay up all night. I'm glad I did not give up.

I got a job and started working at a financial institution right after graduating college. I was so excited and was promoted multiple times. However, even as a young adult, I felt like I was not good enough for anything or anyone. My childhood abandonment from my father kept creeping back into my life as a constant reminder of my limiting belief. I placed my focus on work instead of building meaningful relationships with individuals.

I enjoyed volunteering and found myself being more fulfilled when I gave my time to help others. While working at the financial institution, I volunteered at multiple events. I met a group of women while volunteering, which provided me with a vision that later changed my life.

A Few years after graduating college, I met my husband during my vacation in Florida. We kept our friendship for years. One year during my summer vacation, I came to visit him. I had the best time spending time with him and he seemed to understand me well. He was also an immigrant from Peru and understood what it was like to learn a different culture. I then decided to move to be with him as our relationship became more serious.

One day as I was cleaning out my closet, he told me about his intention to start a family. My immediate reaction was that it would not work as I had no desire to become a mom. I told him that I did not grow up in a perfect family and would not be a good fit to be a mom. What he told me served as a pivotal moment in my life. He advised me to stop being a victim and allow myself to be happy. I was angry at first. I was thinking, "Who is he to tell me that I'm being a victim?" But then I thought hard about this for a few days and I realized he was right. I was being a victim all along and living my present based on my past. I was not allowing myself to be happy and understood that ultimately it is up to me to create my future. I took on this advice and gave it my best to let go of my past. It was not perfect as I was still hanging on to many events, but I did at least allow myself to be happy most of the time.

We got married the same year and shortly after had our first child. The first year was difficult as I was adjusting to my married life and being a new mom. Our second child came a few years after our first. After having my two children, my life changed dramatically and made me refocus on my priorities. I recognized the love I have for my children. I also realized how fortunate I am to have the support from my husband and my husband's family.

My husband is a big self-help fan and we attended multiple seminars including Jack Canfield and Tony Robbins. I learned that life happens for me, not to me. Thinking back, my parents had me when they were both teenagers and they did not have the resources I have now. Also, I tend to remember things how I wanted to remember them, as I was being a victim all this time. I'm certain that things were not as bad as I remembered them to be.

Because of my insecurity, I used to work harder, which helped me excel in school and my career. I graduated with high honors in college and obtained my Masters in Business Administration (MBA) while working full time. This is due to the incredible drive and work ethics I developed from my mom who had high expectations of me.

The relationship between my mom and stepdad improved a great deal after they found religion and my stepdad also stopped gambling. They visit us often and my children adore them. They turned out to be great grandparents. My brother and I talk more often after I moved to the U.S. and he has turned out to be a remarkable man. We have a much better relationship.

I also forgave my father, which wasn't easy at first. I remembered being very angry and wrote him a letter stating that I was disappointed that he left me and my mom when I was little. However, after attending some self-development seminars, I realized that I was hurting myself for holding on to the hate and disappointment. I would not be able to fully experience freedom and joy with the negative emotion.

Putting myself in his shoes, he was very overwhelmed after all the years and meeting me for the first time. He had obligations with his family. I believe that he does have love for me as his child. I also realized that forgiving him really helped me as I allowed myself to be free.

Life was happening for me. As an adult with my own family, looking back now, I realize that if my father had stayed with my mother, they would not have gotten along based on their personalities. I would not have my half brothers and sisters in my life, who turned out to be amazing individuals and parents.

My mentors at work helped me with my growth and encouraged me to challenge myself. I gained confidence by taking on tasks that were outside my comfort zone. Ultimately, I was promoted to be a First Vice President at a leading financial institution in the U.S. While I was grateful for all the opportunities, I felt that my purpose was not fulfilled. After making a radical decision, I stepped down from my role and started Behind those Heels, which was a vision I created over 8 years prior, while volunteering. I was inspired by the group of women I volunteered with.

Getting to know this group of women, I learned that they all went through major challenges, despite their confident appearances. The goal of the organization is to share stories from women who overcame major challenges to inspire others. I also started my firm helping businesses and individuals to achieve financial freedom using my expertise in finance. I feel more alive than ever and love to talk to exceptional women every day while building my network in Behind those Heels.

I wish that my younger self could have read a story like mine, but then I remembered things happened to me for a reason. Life happens for me, not to me. Perhaps I had to experience all the events in the past so I would have the opportunity to share my story. Maybe my story is meant to inspire someone who is going through a similar journey.

Every day is an opportunity to make this world a better place. I'm looking forward to the day when millions of women are joining the Behind those Heels movement and sharing their stories. The world may become less judgmental and allow women to be their authentic selves unapologetically, without shame and guilt. It's a beautiful dream and I couldn't have had this vision without my past. I realized that my past is my biggest gift after all.

Cassie Ferrer
Personal Finance Coach, Podcast Host
Behind those Heels and Numbers Nerd Consulting
United States of America
behindthoseheels.com & numbersnerdconsulting.com

The Girl Who Stopped Laughing

by Ruth Murray

I love to laugh and for years laughter was the *sunshine of my soul*.

When I met my husband Phil, we found we had the same sense of humor, and many times we laughed over the silly little things in life that happened. Mainly the unexpected oversights, that we tend to overlook when we are in a hurry which when we realized, would have us in fits of laughter together.

When I was 27 and pregnant with our third child, my husband Phil died suddenly and that's when life changed dramatically. What had previously been a lovely walk in a meadow, life had now become a dark and foreboding valley.

The years after were filled with toxic relationships until I decided it was time to get my self-respect back. And this is how my journey of rediscovery began. Though it seemed that my story started when my husband died in 1992. When I really think about it, the issues I faced then and for many years after his death, had always been there. I just was not aware of it at the time, because there had never been any situation in which it had reared his ugly head or affected my life.

I felt like my life had turned upside down in an instant. My husband Phil had a massive brain hemorrhage, due to an undiagnosed underlying brain tumor and died two days later.

I didn't know it at the time, but this was the start of a deep soul-searching journey into my life, my mindset, and beliefs.

A journey which took many years and literally sucked the life out of me.

But it was also a journey of rediscovery as to who I really was and whom I was created to be.

In the midst of pain and disillusionment, I found myself and rose from the ashes of a life I was never meant to have lived.

After Phil's death and in the early stages of grief, I felt extremely rejected. Not that he had any control over what happened, but I kept thinking that if he had really loved me, he would not have died. He should have begged God to send him back to me and our children. I certainly would have if it had been me. His death was the first seed of rejection upon which I started to rebuild my life the best way I could.

I had lost my identity when Phil died, which I came to understand was wrapped up in being his wife. Sure, I was still a mother, and I loved it, my children were young, and I was expecting our third child, but I felt lost in my new role as a single mother. I didn't know where I fit. All our friends who had young children like I had were married.

These were couples we would spend time with. Without Phil being there, I felt left out and on the edges of what was once a close circle of friends.

No matter how hard I tried, there was always that empty space beside me. In the end, because these feelings were so hurtful and left me in so much pain and confusion, I withdrew within myself. I changed churches and with it I changed friends.

After nearly two years of being widowed I met my future husband. He was charming, funny, talkative and showered me with love and affection. Within ten days of dating him, he suggested we get engaged, because after all we were adults and there was no reason that he could see why we should wait. Five months later we had tied the knot.

He had no belongings of his own, so he moved into my house. Being the trusting person I am, I signed my bank accounts up with his.

I was so happy, knowing that I belonged to somebody. No more feelings of being alone and isolated. Someone to love me and my children and someone to walk through life with me. An opportunity for me to once again be a wife.

Sadly, my feelings of elation didn't last long. Two days after marrying him, I knew I had made the wrong decision.

Walking along the beach in Rarotonga, bawling my eyes out after his first physical and verbal altercation towards me, had left me shaken and shocked.

As a Christian, I took my vows seriously and in my mind it would not have been acceptable for me to leave. I did love him, so very much and hoped that this was just a one-off incident. Little did I know that this was only the beginning of his abuse and control of not just me, but also my three prior children, and the three children I ended up having with him.

The ten years that followed saw not just me, but my children also, undergo a huge change. Fear of speaking out over issues that came up. Protecting my children in case he attacked them. Being threatened with knives and broken bottles if I spoke up about what was going on in the home, and being slapped and ridiculed in front of my children, reduced me to a woman who felt she was worth nothing. Hating myself for accepting his abuse of me and for not knowing how to get out of this situation as a Christian woman who had vowed to love her husband till death do us part. I became quiet, fearful and any previous days of laughter had become a distant memory.

My children, happy and free when he wasn't home, would become withdrawn and quiet, often hiding in their rooms. We were ruled with an iron fist.

Eventually however, close friends of ours came to see me, when he was at work, and urged me to leave. They knew a little bit of what had been going on, and felt so concerned for myself and the children, that they could no longer stand by and watch his abuse of me.

They gave me the permission from a Christian standpoint, that it was ok to leave and that God, would never expect me to be in a marriage where we were abused. This was not love.

When I found the courage to leave, with their support and a counsellor, I had lost all my friends; I had lost my home due to his excessive spending habits and I was a shadow of my former funny exuberant self. But through all of this, I was grateful to still have all my six children with me.

Although I felt free, I no longer cared about myself, and was left feeling extremely sad. I had done everything to keep everyone happy, but life had failed me. The only ones I genuinely cared about were my children and they became my focus.

It was not long after leaving my marriage, that I got myself involved in another relationship. This relationship though not overtly abusive, was nevertheless toxic and damaging. He couldn't commit and the relationship for the following nine years was all on his terms.

He would stand me up, wanted to spend more time with his ex-wife than me, and whenever I questioned him about it, an argument was sure to follow. I would try harder to be sweeter and more tolerant whilst he continued to disrespect and dishonor me with his continual drug use, not making us a priority and his repeated unfaithfulness. When I finally left, I decided then and there, broken as I was, that I would not enter another relationship again. I was at last ready to start working on me.

As I looked back on my life and reflected on the choices I had made since Phil died.

It felt that ever since his death, my life had been a struggle. I craved the approval of others through the things I did and who I was. Scared to lose those close to me. I believed that if I did all the 'right' things in the eyes of others, I would be approved of. Even if those 'right' things, compromised my values and character.

I was scared of rejection because I did not belong, I tried to do everything I could to belong. But by not living who I truly was, I was disrespected anyway

I was a target to be used by others and I was responsible for that by allowing the disrespect to continue.

Phil had accepted me for who I was and those were four happy years of being content and happy. When he died, I plummeted into a huge identity crisis. I noticed that everything in my life, that made me feel good about myself, came from outside influences. I noticed that my marriages and the need to be in a relationship was what I used to make myself feel good and accepted.

Everything I was and did was based on how others thought of me. My value and worth were packaged in sources, people, and things outside of myself, but it left me with a huge gap in my life. Though that gap was filed with things and feel good vibes, none of that was permanent.

I decided to reclaim my life and took action by making a list of everything I believed about myself and although it was so hard to be reflective with my own life, I chose to continue and persist, despite the pain this gave me.

My children helped me a lot in seeing me as my true self, for who I really was.

They continually affirmed to me that I was a great person. That I was a fun and loving person. Not the mean person like I had been told on so many occasions that I was, if at any given time I had not wanted to do or give something.

My mindset required a lot of work. I didn't consider myself to be a person of worth or value and that showed in how I related to others, especially in relationships.

My driving force was false beliefs that I would gain worth and value through the approval of others. This showed in everything I did, my business, my friends, my relationships, and my family. I just couldn't say no, although I wanted to so many times. I feared that if I said no, they would be angry at me and that would create fear within me. Fear of what they could do to me.

Self-care was unheard of throughout my life. I felt guilty if I did anything for myself or if I spent money on myself. There was a little voice in the back of my mind, telling me I was selfish and greedy. There was a lot of work to be done, yet awareness of how I had been was the biggest step I took towards my healing.

I started to listen to YouTube videos by Trent Shelton 'telling me' that not everyone was in my corner, even if they said they loved me. That talk alone shook me to my core, it was like the blindfold coming off slowly and seeing life from an entirely different perspective. I started to devour as many self-development teachings I could and in conjunction with my bible readings came to see that I was actually quite valuable.

One very helpful technique I used is that I created a list of how I had been treated in the past. It was painful as it was years of hurt and agony that had accumulated in my heart. In doing so I saw the thread of disrespect weave itself in and around my life. Though I was not responsible for how others were, I was responsible for my own actions in it all, although I didn't know any better at the time.

My experiences taught me and confirmed the false beliefs I had formed about myself. The good news was that I could replace those beliefs with a new positive and confident mindset.

Once I had my list of how I had been treated, I wrote down how I wanted to be treated. That was really where the line in the sand was drawn for me. Out of that, came my boundaries, of which I previously had none. I also learned to say no to actions and behaviors I did not appreciate.

The more I did this and changed my experiences with those

around me, the more confident I became. I found my voice and my authenticity, and I could laugh again with all the exuberance I could muster.

I found a new way of dressing, which appealed to me and which became my unique way of being. Prior to that, I always compared myself to others and that I should dress like they did because it would make me look cool.

My negative mindsets over time were replaced with positive beliefs about myself. Every time I made a choice for myself, I felt so good because I was in control of my life without the constant fear, guilt and anxiety of what others thought of me.

And the most special thing that came back to me, was my laughter.

My witty, dry sense of humor showed up once again in my personality.

It felt freeing and fun to once again laugh without reservation.

I continued to focus on self-development and still do to this day. Life is so good now and I know it is because I make conscious choices daily, based on what I know I deserve and am worthy of.

How about you? How about the you who reads this? Have you been in the place where I was? Or are you still there?

Is your worth and value wrapped up in external factors? Have you stopped laughing?

You can be authentic and change the false beliefs that have haunted and directed your life for so long. You don't have to be in a relationship where you are not treated with respect.

You can rise from the ashes just like I did and create a brand new exciting, authentic life, loving whom you were created to be.

It is never ok for someone else to steal your zest for life.

It is never ok to have your laughter taken away.

Live the life you were meant to live with bravery and courage, shining forth your unique personality.

Life taught me that we are the master of our circumstances. We determine how we react to circumstances outside of our control.

We may not be able to stop what comes to us in life, but we do have control over how we respond and what we do with what has been given to us.

Ruth Murray
Coach
Seeds of Change Mindset Coaching
New Zealand
seedsofchangemindsetcoaching.com

The Lies that Caged Me

by Georgia Pomrenke

Have you ever been in a situation where you became someone that you don't even recognize? Or, where you started to develop a pattern of behavior that didn't align with who you are or who you want to be?

In 2014, I noticed that whenever my superiors were questioning each other, my heart would start doing flips, my palms would start to sweat, and my mind would completely shut down. No matter how many times I told myself I was okay, I had to leave the room. As soon as I stepped out of the room, I would feel relief.

I hadn't experienced this before, so I wasn't sure why this was happening to me. Eventually, I realized that I was being triggered—the patterns of my past and the coping skills that correlated with those experiences were surfacing. This was because they removed my sense of safety from my life at that time. I had just moved, and I didn't feel like I had a secure place to land. Therefore, all the "junk" that had been buried started surfacing.

As painful as this journey has been, I am grateful for this experience as it opened my eyes to the mental and emotional abuse I had experienced. I had to work to overcome the abuse of my past before I could get to the root of the mental and emotional abuse I heaped upon myself as a result of my previous experiences.

I'm not a therapist, nor am I a parent. I'm talking about this from my own personal experiences and the perception I had of them—whether my perception was right or wrong—and how it shaped my world view.

During my formative years, my parents were rarely involved in my life. My brother and I had a lot of freedom. We tried to be respectful of the freedom given. Life was good, for the most part. I felt happy, confident, secure, and able. My world view was rocked around 4th grade when my parents became overly focused on my weight and how I looked. My parents put me on various diet pills and took me to Weight Watchers with them—this was when fake sugars and low-fat everything was being heavily pushed.

They started hover-parenting me around food and activity. I realize now that this came from a place of love and desire to see me succeed—to not be ridiculed and made fun of by my peers, and to set me up for a better future. At the time, I couldn't see that. They relied on me to figure all of this out on my own. They relied on other people to tell me what to do, and they didn't give me an example to follow.

Reminder, this is from my perspective. I feel like I need to mention this again.

I started to spiral. In my mind, the parents who used to say I could do or be anything I put my mind to no longer believed that. I was no longer beautiful in their eyes — not really. The guilt and shame I now felt over my looks crushed me like a heavy weight. I became ashamed and afraid. I quit the swim team, stopped doing anything that was "in front of people," and stopped playing during recess — choosing activities that made me invisible. In addition to what was happening internally, the food I was eating — all those fake sugars, low-fat carbs, etc. — left me feeling tired all the time; and, for the first time in my life, I was developing a "tire" around my belly.

Unfortunately, I didn't understand, nor did I have enough of a developed relationship with my parents to talk about what I was going through. This patten continued to worsen. Whatever fad diet my parents chose to follow, what worked for my dad was expected to work for me. I'd feel the harsh judgement of every food choice. I'd feel every word said when I wanted to eat more than one meal a day when my parents decided that that was the best way to lose weight. And on…and on… My whole world became shame and fear for many years.

I felt like I was punished using food and rewarded or comforted using food. Eventually I had to understand that my parents were doing the best they could with what they knew and understood.

At some point I had to realize that if I wanted open communication with my parents, then I had to be willing to take a risk and be open with them and asking questions when I didn't understand what they were trying to say. So, I took that leap in 2017. The good news is that I now have a great, open relationship with my parents—they never gave up on me, and I never gave up on them. But it took me a long time to get there. And now I have to figure out all of the false beliefs and fears that were gleaned from the world around me through these experiences.

I haven't completely broken my "cage" here. I find that there are many layers I have to break through in order to become the person I want to be because my childhood was riddled with other types of emotional and mental abuse that I had to overcome and continue to work on. I want to share some of my own personal strategies with you to support you in your journey that I have gleaned from life's challenges since 2014.

1. **Silent Treatment and Cold Shoulder:** In spite of negative behavior or negative consequences from actions taken, people need to feel connected. Connecting and communicating after a bad decision or negative consequences doesn't cause a person to want to do it again and again (unless they have deeper issues than what I am qualified to discuss here). There's no need for this type of behavior.

    When I did something I *knew* I shouldn't have done, I expected this. I would be perfectly okay with this because I *knew* I was in the wrong. But, not talking through it with my parents left me feeling isolated from them and the rest of the family. When I didn't do anything to deserve it or didn't know that a specific thing was expected of me to do, this behavior silenced me and made me feel like I wasn't an important part of the family.

2. **Hover Parenting and Micromanaging:** We all need the

ability to make choices in life and be able to experience the consequences of those choices—good or bad. It's called dignity of risk. When things are done *for* us instead of us having that opportunity, it takes away our power and doesn't allow us to grow. I see this one *a lot* in families and even in the workplace between supervisors and employees. Shoot, I even do it without realizing when I'm at work.

If you realize yourself doing this, one effective tip I would share to overcome this is to start with something you're scared of allowing another to do. Ask yourself:
- Why am I scared?
- Is there anything that I can do to work my way up to allowing someone else to make the choice?

It's all about baby steps—but you have to be willing to go there, and you have to be willing to let go of having control.

3. **Manipulation.** The game of life is a game of manipulation and everyone has their own "superpower" or "go-to" move with this. You can use your superpower for good or for evil.

Here are a few of the narcissistic ones I've encountered:
   a. "If you loved/liked/respected me, you would ...."
   b. No words—just glares, huffs, and eye rolls.
   c. Not seeing the value in who or what someone is becoming—only seeing the direction planned for you; and, because of this, you're treated like a disappointment.
   d. Not seeing someone's growth—continually throwing past mistakes in their face.
   e. When trying to process something out loud or ask questions because you need a moment, and the person *controlling* the situation shuts you down with one of the following:

i. Topic changed to interrupt your thought process so that they can have the last word.
   ii. "Well, then I'll just go .... (whatever it was they were asking you to do after you started asking for clarification on how to do it)."
   iii. The silent, brooding face until you just feel stupid and stop talking.
   iv. Frequently interrupt (not because they're excited but because *'they know more'*) and/or talking over you while withholding key information that would actually help you process. Or the flip side to this: interrogating in a way that shuts you down because you don't have the thoughts or visuals to process everything being thrown at you. This is a form of bullying—one of the more accepted forms.
5. **The Blame Game:** This is a hard one to differentiate between people simply asking questions to find out what went wrong and people looking for someone to blame for something that happened. Sometimes it's not any one person's fault—in fact, it's almost always a little bit of everyone's fault.

   It's about how do we make this better? How do we move forward together? If this is not part of the conversation, then proceed with caution. Never stay in a situation where you, as the victim, carry the blame in a negative situation or condition you find yourself in. *Get out* as soon as you can. You are worthy, deserving, and capable of so much more without all of that.
6. **Joking or being over-critical:** For years, my dad, and then my brother thought it was fun to constantly make fun of me about everything: how I dressed, what I said, what I did, how I ate,

how I moved, etc., etc. I played along with it for quite some time. But when it became the only conversation they had with me, I stopped "handling it." When it ended in tears (on my end), I still got made fun of for crying, or worse, got yelled at and told that I needed to stop crying or stop being such a baby. I know that by now you may be *feeling* me right now and know exactly what I'm talking about.

Throughout the years, some days, I could take it, some days, I couldn't. However, today, my husband makes me laugh a lot with his playful teasing which pulls me out of overly-sensitive funks I find myself in. He knows my past and stops when I ask because he loves me and never wants me to feel less than or marginalized because I have childhood trauma in this particular area. I'm thankful for this show of love and respect from him every day.

What I've Learned

I have learned so much from my experiences growing up, including how I have created my own cage by internalizing the coping mechanisms created from my childhood experiences. The people around me now are nothing like the experiences I listed above; although, how I interpret behaviors and words is clouded by these past experiences.

I have learned that I now have to stop and assess every time I have an emotional response to figure out if what I am experiencing is real or of the past. To do that, I have to look at the *whole picture*—not just the moment. I have to ask questions, no matter how scared I might be of the answers I may receive.

Beloved, if this all sounds familiar to you and you had similar childhood experiences, you may have a child's heart inside you crying out for acceptance, love, and healing from these hurts. I challenge you with a few thoughts to journal to support your healing.

1. What is it that you started to believe about yourself and how you relate to the world *after* you became aware of this?
2. Who told you what you had to be in this moment?
3. How did you change, capitulate, or morph into something you were never meant to be?
4. How has that affected you every day?
5. What can you do for yourself to support your own healing?

Another great exercise I learned from my therapist that has supported me significantly is the following visualization.

1. Close your eyes and visualize yourself at the age when you first lost faith in yourself or others. See the beautiful, innocent child you were.
2. Ask your inner child what they want to tell you right now and listen.
3. Write the answers down.
4. Then, say to your inner child *"I am done telling you that you are not enough. You are more than enough. I am done telling you that you are unlovable because you are loved unconditionally, and you are beautiful."*
5. Journal about your experience and do this as many times as you need to in order to heal.

Once you figure this out and it gets tough, don't stop—you'll eventually find yourself on the other side of it, living the life you've always wanted to live.

You now have a choice to continue as you have been, or to embrace this as *your* new journey.

Georgia Pomrenke
VP of Human Resources
SIRS, Inc.
United States of America
georgiamarie3333.com

Mindset, Magic, and Manifestation

by Michelle Montero

There I was, celebrating my first four figure day in my business. Hard to imagine that less than a year ago, I was homeless and living in my car with my fiancé and our four cats.

I remember it so well. It still shrinks my heart when I think about it. I can still remember my panic and dread at the thought of waking up and finding one of my cats suffocated because it was so *hot* in that car.

I remember the sound of my fiancé crying in the middle of the night in anguish of what had become of our lives. I remember how bad my stomach hurt from practically starving. I remember having to choose between feeding ourselves or feeding our pets. There was always that horrible pain in my gut. You know, like when that big ball grows in your throat and the sound of your heart pounds in your ears because it hurts to see the ones you love suffer so much. I would have given anything to just wake up and realize it was all just a nightmare, but it was really my reality.

After being homeless and living in the car and a tent for a few months, I developed an anger for my situation. I was tired of people ignoring my existence because they thought I was going to ask them for money. That was one of the things I absolutely refused to do—become a beggar. As hungry as I was, and as dirty as I was, I wouldn't dare ask anyone for money, for food or for personal hygiene items.

One day, my car battery died after keeping it running with the air conditioning on for so long. It was around summer time when we were homeless and it was so hot. I remember feeling so broken, hopeless, and angry. My cats were suffocating in the car and I was starting to panic. It's honestly them in the end who gave me the will power and the determination to get the hell out of that situation and become financially stable again.

I can still feel the emptiness in my stomach from starving every day, and the tightness in my throat from crying. It became clear, if I wanted to get out of this, I needed to swallow my pride and *ask for HELP!* You see, the way I was raised, I would rather be caught dead than have anyone find out about my homelessness.

My family didn't find out about it until the very end. I'm sure, if I had swallowed my pride and asked for help from the beginning, I wouldn't have been in that pickle for such a long time.

If you're unable to do something by yourself, do not be afraid to ask for help. We have friends and family for a reason—for support. Let your friends and family support you when you need them. Be open to *receiving*.

You must be wondering, how does someone become homeless? Well, for us, becoming homeless wasn't a choice, it happened as a result of a series of events, from illegal evictions and not being able to work effectively because I was living in my car 24/7, unable to have a shower or cook for myself.

Everything changed for us when my fiancé's family who at the time owned a bodega store, which was the bread and butter for the family as it provided a consistent income to support everyone. My fiancé also worked there for five years, until the family decided to sell the store when his grandfather became ill and could no longer manage the store in the summer of 2017. This led to the family falling on hard times, including food being in short supply in their home.

We all lived there and when you are trying to start a family of your own in a full house, it wasn't ideal for my fiancé and I. We decided to move to Florida for a new start in the summer of 2018 and then suddenly ended up moving back to New Jersey to avoid the devastation that was expected from hurricane Michael.

We left everything behind in the hope to either avoid being caught in the hurricane or to come back and pick up where we left off. I was working from home for a company doing a call center job, and when we moved back to New Jersey to stay at my fiancé's family's house that had more than 15 people living there, it became impossible for me to do that job. It was just too noisy.

After that, I wasn't able to earn enough money to take the road trip back to Florida and by then the landlord had already thrown all my things out of the apartment which was an illegal eviction.

His grandfather wasn't getting any better and we were told that our four cats were causing him an allergic reaction. So, we were asked to leave with very little notice. We didn't have anywhere to go and we couldn't bring all of our belongings with us. We were trying really hard to avoid actually being homeless so we found this homesteading program. This is a program where a person volunteers to work and learn on a farm in exchange for hospitality like a warm bed to sleep in and 3 square meals daily.

We took our first road trip to a farm in Illinois where we stayed for about three weeks learning about sustainability and agriculture. I'm talking a farm with a lake, horses, alpacas, cows, chickens, pigs, a hay barn, and an outhouse!

We learned how to tend to a greenhouse, vegetable beds, how to make bread, how to thread alpaca hair into fabric. We were really enjoying the experience and learning a lot, then things started to get weird with the arrangement, so we decided to leave for our own safety.

We found ourselves back in New Jersey again with nowhere to go and that's when our homelessness began.

My experiences have left me being even more driven to never abandon my family or let them down. I am the oldest sibling and so I have this strong sense of loyalty and determination. I'm inspired by my family, my pets, and loved ones to fight for a better tomorrow every single present day. They inspire me to not only provide for them but to become stronger, both physically and mentally so that I can better take care of them, at all costs.

Some of the challenges I've had to face were very much themed around dualism, and mostly during my late childhood years to my young adult years. For a long time, I struggled with a large range of mental health issues. From the early age of twelve, I've struggled with depression, anxiety, and other intense emotions.

At thirteen, I had to learn how to trust again after being sexually assaulted which practically ripped me apart. I had to struggle with making a sacrifice that almost tore my family apart by telling them the truth so that I could start healing and trusting again.

By the time I was fifteen I was struggling with my demons, substance abuse and impulsive dangerous behaviors, all unsafe coping mechanisms that I had developed to help me cope with my life and the phases that I was going through.

After disconnecting from my hometown of New Jersey at seventeen, I started to change and grow a feeling of longing to *go home*. I also developed an interest and calling to the metaphysical. My spiritualism began to grow and this is where I began to see the dualism in my challenges.

I've come to recognize that my challenges stem from a complete human and egotistic experience. What I mean is, when I learned and started to accept the oneness of everything that exists and tune into all the frequencies around me, I realized this is all bigger than just me. It's completely macro, and it allowed me to distance myself and view my past pain and suffering from a different perspective.

I realized that I'm not just a human with a lot of intense emotions because I have mental health issues or because I'm crazy. I had all these intense emotions because I was meant to go through tribulations that would ignite my gifts.

We have to go through challenges to become stronger and find our true selves in the end. I only learned this after I was given the opportunity to lose everything I thought I loved in 2019. I guess I was pretty materially consumed and had lost my respect for the fact that others work for something just as hard as I do. It started with losing my home and all my belongings, including memories (journals, yearbooks, photo albums, personal art drawings showing my intimate progression through my life). I felt like I lost a part of who I was.

In 2019, I thought my world was falling apart. I was invisible to the community and drowning in my sadness and self-pity. Every day I would just wonder when it would all be over.

One day, I talked with a friend who shared that she was in our shoes before and said that we will get out of the situation. She shared a lot of tips with me, and gave me a tent, a water cooler and some snacks to take on our hunt for a place to camp out. Our car was starting to give out. She also told me about a few local resources I wasn't aware of, like the Homeless Coalition. The Homeless Coalition turned out to be another life saver.

I don't think my friend will ever know how much of an impact she had on my life that day. I was at my lowest point. I was completely fed up with our situation and not being able to eat meals or take showers was tough. When your daily basic needs aren't met, it becomes something so draining to the soul. It was hurting me to see my fur babies in such awful conditions, and I wanted to do more for them.

The Homeless Coalition helped us by giving us a hotel voucher for a while so that we could have a warm bed, a hot shower, and warm meals while we were working. It was extremely hard to work delivery gigs and live in the car—you gotta keep the AC on in the summer. Also, eating out for every meal because you don't have a kitchen hurts the pocket. We were extremely grateful to have the help of the Homeless Coalition.

And of course, my parents helped us too. They helped pitch in with any additional funds, as the vouchers had a deadline. With the support from the Homeless Coalition and my family, having a place to think allowed us to get back on our feet again. I got back to work and quickly started learning about building a business in the online space.

I decided to invest in a business coach and it was a complete life and game changer. I started learning about mindset blocks and money blocks. I started the shadow work to open myself up to healing, abundance and happiness. That's how my beliefs began to transform.

Today, I'm a whole new person. I put my personal development and self-care first. I started my first business from scratch, becoming the first business owner in my entire immediate and distant family. I officially celebrated my first four figure day!

Don't underestimate yourself and remember your current state does not reflect or determine your final destination.

I think one of the main themes in my life story so far is to persevere, to believe in something bigger than me. I used to have a lot of negative self-talk and limiting beliefs, and that all started to dissipate after I made it my responsibility to grow and heal inside. I started expressing more gratitude, looking at the situation from a positive view point, meditating and doing things to just feed my soul.

When I took a step back and allowed myself the time to heal my soul, I slowly started to see my perspective about the world change. My limiting beliefs started to develop into positive beliefs. I took a once undisciplined and reckless routine and developed it into my daily morning ritual, and if I miss just one of my soul feeding activities, I notice the difference throughout my day.

It's only been one year since I was homeless in 2019. I really don't know where my journey will take me, but what I know for sure is that it will only get better. I am a firm believer that sometimes we will face trials and tribulations to prepare and humble us for the marvelous things that are to come.

Although 2019 was practically a nightmare, there was so much growth involved that I see now it was for a much bigger purpose. I didn't experience homelessness as a punishment or because I was a bum. I experienced it because I needed to become humble so that when I do attract all my wealth and abundance, it doesn't go to my head.

We've all heard stories about good people changing for the bad because of money. I know that my experience was meant to spark a sincere appreciation and gratitude inside of my heart. I want my experience to show that money can spark a positive change. I made a promise to God that if I did make it out of my homelessness, that whatever wealth and abundance I earn will also be passed along to help the homeless prevention system.

This journey has taught me so much. One of the greatest lessons has been that I learned how important it is to be humble, be resourceful, and still ask for help when you need it. I wasn't educated about resources available to me, and because I was so embarrassed about my situation, I didn't ask for help or guidance. That help and guidance saved my life and my family's life.

I am sharing my story because I have a deep calling that I can no longer ignore. I want to help everyone create a purposeful life full of joy and abundance in all areas of their life. I want to prove that when you do things out of love, only the best things will come — not just for you but for those around you and the universe too. I want this to start a ground shaking ripple effect that will ultimately raise the collective conscious vibration and heal our world.

It is easy to sit back and allow the fear to take over. However, my experiences have allowed me to feel the fear and pain of not reaching my dreams and staying stuck in a situation I didn't want to be in. Feel the anxiety and discomfort of not knowing what to do or how to get out of a situation, and then finding hope. Knowing that there is still a way, even if you don't know it or you can't see it yet for yourself.

I want you to feel excited for what's possible in the future and fall in love with the feeling of what it will be like when you finally accomplish the BIG goal for your big WHY.

I have finally started manifesting my desires and goals in life while it's still fresh in my mind. I'm only 6 months into my business and seeing wonderful results. I want to share how I got those results so others can start implementing and manifesting their dream life too.

Everyone knows the saying that *'money is the best way to make a difference'*. Well, I want to be that difference and be remembered for helping people who are facing financial hardships and homelessness. To find the light at the end of the tunnel, build something out of nothing - a business - something that they can make a living with, and in the long run, fill hearts with hope.

I've never felt a greater desire or energy than that of wanting to put peace, hope and love in the hearts of those feeling empty, alone, and afraid.

Michelle Montero
Marketing Strategist
Michelle Montero
United States of America
michellemontero.us

Living and Thriving with Depression

by Debbie Brady

His words made me tear up because they were so accurate and so powerful.

In his NFL Hall of Fame speech, former Philadelphia Eagles, Brian Dawkins, openly discussed his struggle with depression and suicidal thoughts that he had early in his career. He spoke to all of us who have battled depression or lived with depression at various times when he said, "*So for those who are going through it right now, there is hope. You do have hope. There is something on the other side of this. Don't be caught up where you are. Don't stay where you are. Keep moving. Keep pushing through.*"

Whenever I am struggling with my depression, I have always held onto the hope knowing things will get better once I get to the other side.

I have been living with depression since I was fifteen, and

honestly, most likely since I was even younger.

At the end of the day, I think we can all agree that depression sucks! Really sucks! Like, down to your bones, hurts your heart and soul kind of sucks. For some, depression is a passing phase; a single episode that goes away, never to return after it is addressed and treated.

For others, myself included, it is like that unwanted guest that comes for a visit unannounced and overstays their welcome. When it finally moves on, you hope it never comes to visit again, yet it almost always does.

Growing up, I was a shy and quiet child, to the point of being completely withdrawn at times. I have always had friends, but was never super social. Large crowds overwhelmed me, they still overwhelm me when they are indoors. Even recess was challenging. I was just never sure how to break into a group of kids or how to best make conversation, but it was all I knew how to be. I have always been a people pleaser, to the point of hurting myself in the hopes of helping someone else or, at least have them like me.

I have always struggled with feelings of insecurity and feeling like I was never very smart. These feelings of insecurity and incompetence eventually led to feelings of sadness and depression as I went through puberty and into the middle of my teenage years. In high school, my shyness persisted, but I was slowly becoming more comfortable with those I knew.

I went to a small school system in suburban Philadelphia, so by high school, I had been in school with the same group of kids since kindergarten. Even though I wasn't friends with most of them, we all knew each other pretty well and there was a certain comfort level for me. I had a good group of friends and always had someone to sit with at lunch or pair up with in class, so I was rarely alone. Yet, I had a constant feeling of loneliness and emptiness inside. I had zero self-confidence.

I look back and my memories of those years and I realize I was more of a spectator than a participant in the world around me. Being social simply took more energy than my mind had. When I went off to college, just a week after graduation from high school, I made a conscious decision to 'come out of my shell' and no longer be shy. It was a new start in a place where no one really knew me. I decided I would say "yes" to social opportunities such as parties, and campus activities. I wanted to force myself to go out there and meet people and to be a participant in my life and not just an observer.

It worked, but it also took its toll. I didn't address any of my insecurities and low self-esteem. I didn't acquire any coping skills or internal strength so I wasn't really changed inside. It was really more of like putting on a Band-Aid. With the change of graduating high school, starting college and then the impending demise of my parents' marriage, my first severe bout of depression began to descend upon my mind and body in the fall of 1986, when I was 17. My life was about to change in many ways, but it would take me years to fully accept these changes and to be able to fully embrace who I was physically and mentally.

The fall of 1986 began the start of the darkest and most difficult time in my life. I honestly was not sure I would make it to the other side, but by the grace of God and some amazing loved ones, I made it.

During this time, I fell deeper into the depths of depression than I had known was even possible. My depression was so severe that I lost my appetite completely, which quickly led to rapid weight loss and a diagnosis of depression and Anorexia. At 5'7", my weight went from 130 pounds down to 84 pounds in a matter of a few months. By the time I went to the doctor for help, they told me I was only a few pounds away from death. They treated me for anorexia and that was the main focus of my therapy sessions. What my family and doctor didn't understand was that the Anorexia was a symptom of my depression and not the cause of it.

In fact, it took me years to realize my main challenge in life would be with managing my depression and not my eating disorder. Maybe it was what we focused on at the time, because it was easier to measure my progress and visibly see the healing. Whereas with depression, it is harder to physically see if someone is improving, and easier for them to fake it.

The fact that I did not understand at the time that depression was a health issue I needed to learn more about—and find coping skills to manage—resulted in lost time and years of suffering more than I needed to. I kept thinking I just wasn't fully better yet, or that my depression would go away and this would be the final time. But that was never the case.

What I realized by the end of my 20s, was that depression was a health condition I would have to learn to manage and live with for the rest of my life. I began to look into things that could help me. My degrees are in psychology, and I received my masters in counseling in 1994, so I did have a lot of theoretical knowledge and understanding on depression and how to treat others on a therapeutic level. All of this knowledge was great for my intended profession in the mental health world. However, it wasn't enough to help me in the day-to-day battle against depression in my life.

So, in my late 20s, I began to look at activities and ways of life that would help me live a more productive and happy life, including therapy.

I also learned how society and others look at depression and mental health in general, and how we need to continue to educate society and end the stigma that seems to still attach itself to mental illness.

The two times in my life where my depression was at its worse, was during my teens when my puberty hormones were changing, and then in my mid-late 40s as I went through menopause. This, along with some physical symptoms, led me to reassess some of my former ways of dealing with my depression. At the same time, I also began to experiment with some new strategies that ended up helping both my depression and my physical symptoms. As I learned more about my physical condition, I learned that the two were interrelated.

Depression is part of who I am, but it does NOT define who I am any more than any other disease defines anyone. However, I have had to accept that it is something I will always deal with and have had to learn to manage.

My mind simply struggles on certain days. Over the years, I have learned that there are certain activities I can do in order to help keep my depression away, as well as better ways to cope with it when it makes an appearance. Exercising, eating clean, whole foods, living in a warm, sunny climate, taking antidepressants, having someone to talk to, and therapy to name a few. It is a constant effort each day and when I slack on these items, I will start to notice.

I wanted to share a few things I wish I had known about living with depression earlier in my journey. Over the years, certain life events and choices I made affected my ability to fully manage my mental health at as high of a level as I need to in order to live my life to my best ability. It also affected my ability to be fully prepared to deal with my ever-changing moods.

First, my depression during my teens wasn't temporary, but rather a chronic mental illness. I was going to have to learn how to manage it throughout my life.

It took me years to figure it out and took me years to accept that this major episode at age seventeen was not just a passing phase. Rather, the beginning of a life-long illness that would go into remission, but would have to be addressed again and again, yet, would get easier once I put a good plan of my own together. I wasted a lot of years hoping that my depression would just "go away" instead of accepting that it was something I was simply going to learn more about and come up with a plan for it and my life.

Second, you aren't alone. For years, I thought I was the only one who struggled with depression. Of course, this was back in the late 80s, long before the internet made our world much smaller. Depression is very isolating by nature. However, it helps so much to know we aren't alone and that thousands of others battle this illness too.

Third, learn all you can about depression. The more educated you are about depression, the better you can learn how to manage it when it hits. Read books, search mental health blogs, watch TED talks, talk to experts and peers and just absorb the knowledge so you have it when you need it and you can create a plan of how to live and thrive despite your depression.

There have been many times that I felt like I just didn't have the strength to make it through the next day or even the next hour. If you have ever felt this way, please remember that you can do it and you will do it. Use your resources to lean on during these times. We are survivors—all of us. Depression doesn't have to win and fully take over our life. You can learn how to manage it and be the one who is stronger. Don't ever forget that you have more strength inside than you can imagine. You are strong and you are worthy.

Please don't ever give up. Please don't ever stop fighting. Please keep pushing through the dark times, because there is always light on the other side. There will be easier times ahead and as you continue to learn and understand your depression and what helps you, you will begin to feel more prepared, more in control, and have more confidence and hope to move through the tougher days.

I have learned so much over the years and yes, I still struggle—daily. However, with each episode of depression I have, I *know* I will come out on the other side even stronger.

By leaning what activities help my depression and mental health, and working hard each day. Helping others understand their own depression and what activities can help them feel stronger, and by continuing to research new techniques that can help depression, I have gotten to a place in life where I am more confident and stronger when my depression hits.

I hope you are able to find the resources that help you. We are stronger together and we aren't alone on this journey.

Debbie Brady
Author, Mental Health Blogger, Content Creator
Ending Stigma Together, LLC
United States of America
endingstigmatogether.com

Becoming Me

by Tania Hunter-Gilligan

I was 20 when I met him. I fell for him because he was *mysterious*. Interesting that thirteen years later when I started studying psychology, I learned that the very thing that attracts us to someone we are not normally attracted to is the same thing that repels us when it ends. I learned just how true this was when the 'mysteriousness' I fell for became 'secretiveness', which ultimately pushed me away.

He was completely different from who I was normally attracted to, he had dark hair, dark skin and dark eyes. I usually liked guys who had fair skin, and blue eyed, the Scandinavian types with the boy next door look. He carried a briefcase and wore a shirt and tie to work. I swore I would never be with a man who was exactly what he was. It never dawned on me to ask myself why I was attracted to him. I just followed something inside me.

Looking back, I see our relationship was based on an idealistic picture of what we wanted our life to look like. I fell in love with this, not the person. I wanted to be married with four kids, have our own home, and live happily ever after. He wanted the same. It was a perfect fit.

We were together for a year before he proposed. We were engaged for two years and were married after three years together. Little did I know then, I married a man like my father, and I transferred all my troubling childhood fears of my father onto my new husband.

I was following a pattern and not a very empowering pattern.

I remember clearly in the months after we were married, watching our wedding video over and over again and bawling my eyes out. It never once occurred to me I had made a decision out of idealism and not out of love. I put it down to missing my mom and being homesick. We lived hundreds of kilometers away from home in Auckland, New Zealand, so I told myself that was why.

So, I got on with married life. A year later became a mom, and I loved being a mom to our son. Giving to him became my focus. He was a happy baby, so it made it easy to be the best mum. Despite some early feeding issues, motherhood was a very happy time for me and I placed all my energy into being the best mom I could be.

Then we moved from Auckland to Hamilton. The move wasn't to Wellington like my husband had promised when we first got married. I always wanted to go back home, to be near my parents, and my family. This is something he promised we would do, yet it wasn't meant to be, yet.

The house was small, moldy, damp and cold, which reflected my emotional state and feelings of hopelessness. The people were friendly, so I focused on meeting new people through playgroup with my son. I became pregnant with our second child. This time around, I felt miserable. I found it hard to hide how unhappy I was. It was not the marriage I thought it would be. He spent weeks away from home working. We had very little money, and I had a sneaky suspicion my husband was spending a lot of money on himself, taking it away from our family budget.

Our second son was born when I was unwell with the flu, in the beginning of winter. His birth was hard, and for the first eight months he cried a lot. It was only then that I realized just how lonely and unhappy I was. When my husband was away for three weeks out of four working, I was left on my own to deal with a sick baby who spent most nights crying. He had developed Bronchiolitis from three months old, and came down with chest illnesses regularly. Later, this developed into asthma.

I started to take my blinkers off, as I began to see the reality of his financial deception. I had no power in our relationship. I was left to budget on very little money, while my husband spent his own money plus dipped into our housekeeping money. I still remember going to the supermarket with a budget and a calculator, knowing exactly how much was in the account. Then getting to the check out and the card declining, only to realize my husband had taken money out of our account again. This happened over and over again, nothing changed, despite my pleading with him. I felt powerless.

I had enough and I finally gained the courage to tell him that I wanted to go to Wellington to stay with my parents for a while. He must have known I wasn't happy and was on the verge of leaving him because he told me I could go but was not going to take the kids. I had a 2-year-old and a breastfed 2-week-old. There was no way I was leaving my babies behind. So I stayed and reluctantly agreed to marriage counselling.

We moved again, it was another rental, another cold house with no money to pay for heating. I got pregnant again, this time though, I lost our baby and that broke my heart. It was the girl I wanted so badly. I was miserable and felt even lonelier.

One day, I was noticed by another man, our security alarm installer. He gave me the attention I was craving. He spent time with me, and seemed really interested in me. Maybe I was naive. I seemed to miss the cues, but then I wasn't looking for them. Then came the day I noticed he wanted more than just friendship. I understood then that he probably did this to all the stay at home mums whose husbands were away. I didn't care about that though, I loved the attention. I felt wanted, sexy, even cherished for a little bit, and I was very tempted. But I didn't let him take it any further. I couldn't, I was too loyal. Despite being terribly unhappy, I couldn't bear to betray my husband, so I said no and I made the decision to tell my husband.

What I saw then should have been the point that I walked away from my marriage, but I didn't. I wasn't strong enough. My husband went into a rage, screaming about how he was going to ruin him, tell his partner, tell his boss and ruin his life. I was in shock. More at the way he wanted to 'ruin' this man in a manipulative way, instead of approach him in a mature way. Yet I still wasn't strong enough to leave.

We moved again, into our third rental, and our third son was born. This time we were living in the country, on a dairy farm. I started to feel happier. I was enjoying motherhood with my placid and happy baby, his two older brothers, and the beauty and peacefulness that living in the country surrounded by gentle cows brings. I was still lonely, but I focused on being a mom, growing a garden, preserving and baking. I actually enjoyed when my husband was away and started to dread when he returned.

We moved a fourth time. This time a 30-minute drive from the children's school. It was still in the country, but it was in a small country village. We had neighbors, so our privacy and peace was gone, but I connected with a lovely elderly neighbor, who loved the children. I fell pregnant again which I knew would be our last baby.

I remember a visit from my parents. They were travelling home from a holiday and spent a couple of days with us. They had both been aware of my husband's spending habits for a while now. My father had tried to help him in the past, without success. He knew I was unhappy and saw my powerlessness. He told my husband to give him his credit card, and when he gave it to him, he cut it up in front of him. It was a surreal feeling for me. I felt good knowing my father was standing up for me, and that we may finally be financially better off. I was very wrong, nothing changed. I found out later he had the card replaced behind my back.

I would look back on this later and realize I had gone from one powerful man to another, without growing my own strong backbone. My relationship with my father would eventually morph into a beautiful equal friendship in later years, as I would learn to step into my power. Right now though, it felt good to know my father had my back.

We moved again, this time back to the area we were before our last move. Closer to the children's school, and on a dairy farm. It was another very damp, moldy and cold house. This is where our fourth and last baby, and our first and only daughter was born.

I still remember the night I went into labor with her. My husband had spent the evening in his office, as he always did, then headed to bed. I told him I was having contractions. He told me to wake him when it was 'time', and fell asleep. I labored for a few hours on my own, before he got up in the early hours to take me to the birthing center. It was then that I realized how much I actually did on my own. I had spent seven years raising babies on my own.

Our daughter was born, and she was a demanding baby. The arguments and power struggles with my husband intensified. I wanted to be seen, to be supported, to be loved, and to be cherished. I felt betrayed, and lied to as he kept secrets from me. I had lost all trust in him, and in our relationship, and the worst part, I felt so incredibly powerless.

I remember a time so vividly when my daughter was a couple of weeks old. Our souls connected so deeply for a moment. We saw each other. I felt she really knew me and knew what I desired. I looked deep into her eyes and I felt her say to me *"It's okay mommy, I'm here now, you can do what you need to do."* I knew at a soul level what she meant. I just didn't know how I could leave her father. I felt I had nowhere to go, and no safety net.

Sixteen months later we were told we had to move again by the landlord, who wanted to move into the home. The difficulties of only renting means we were at the mercy of landlords wanting to sell or have family move in.

I was driven by an unknown inner force this time. I told my husband we were not moving into another rental in the Waikato. I wanted to go home, to be with my family. I knew my parents were looking for a rental. I suggested I ask them if they could buy a rental for us to live in. He reluctantly agreed.

My parents found a home for us an hour north of Wellington on the coast, close to my sister. We moved all our belongings. I moved in to our new home with our children, while my husband stayed in Hamilton until he had found a job in our area, and could leave his job.

I spent eight weeks with my children, in our new home, surrounded by support from my family. I reveled in the time, the space, the quiet contemplation time. I got a cleaning job through my sister while my children were at kindergarten and sent the money to my husband to pay his board.

Ironically here I was, with apparent freedom, and yet I was working to pay his board, while attempting to make ends meet with the little amount of money we had to pay the bills, while my husband continued to live the same lifestyle, and spend money on what he wanted. The last straw came when I found out he hadn't even told his employer we had moved, and was not looking for a new job.

The time on my own opened up a whole new world of realizations for me. How much power I now had, how much happier I was without him. And the biggest one, that I didn't even love him. I found myself asking so many questions, the biggest one, *'had I ever loved him?'* It was a time of emotional turmoil, but also a time of immense clarity. I knew I wanted to leave my husband, I just didn't know how. I leaned on my family, talking over what would be the right thing to do for all.

My father took it the hardest. He didn't understand why I could consider leaving. How could he? He had been with mom since they were teenagers. They were soulmates.

The hardest part was feeling responsible for how my decision would impact my children. Then again, I knew I was not helping them by staying in a marriage when I was miserable. How was that teaching them to follow their heart, to do what is true for themselves?

My decision was made when my husband stayed with us for the Easter break. I felt nothing but the desire to have him out of my life. I made my decision then. I would leave him. I told him I could no longer be with him and I didn't love him.

That's when the real work began. Dealing with his hurt, his anger, and his manipulation. Supporting my children through their father leaving. Seeing who my real friends and support networks were after twelve years with this man. Most importantly, stepping into my power, realizing who I am and finally feeling free.

I would love to have bottled that feeling. The sense of freedom. Knowing I was the creator of my own life now. I could now make my own decisions. I could raise my children how I wanted, knowing if I made mistakes, they were all mine. I could spend my money on what I wanted, without guilt, and without needing permission.

The next two years were extremely challenging. A long legal battle over custody, as I fought to keep the children together and he wanted the opposite. In the end, the children were kept together, and their security remained as intact as we could.

Eighteen years since making the decision to leave my marriage, I look back on it now and I don't recognize the woman I was. I was passive, insecure, and afraid to be myself. I was holding it all in because I didn't think I deserved any better.

Today I am proud of the woman who was brave enough to say *"no more"* and to finally step away from a situation that was stifling me, destroying me, and breaking me. I am now strong, resilient, married to the love of my life and living a full, happy, and purposeful life. My children are all adults, well balanced and independent, and well aware of their parent's strengths and weaknesses.

I still wonder if I would have been able to make the decision without the love and support from the people I had in my life at the time. Maybe I would have. I know I was ready. Sometimes though, all we need is for someone to say *'it's okay, I've got your back"*, and somehow, we find the strength within us to do what we need to do. Show up for ourselves and be the best version of ourselves, even though it's really hard. In the end it's the hardest paths travelled that brings us the biggest rewards. I am living proof of how true that is.

Tania Hunter-Gilligan
CEO, Founder & Holistic Wellness Ambassador
Ignite Your Soul
New Zealand

Find your voice

by Sara Olson

Feelings of dread, disillusion, and grief swept over me as I stared at the ceiling of that old damp historical rented home. He had just driven off.

My 5-year-old daughter and 3-year-old son looked at me with despair. At the age of 25 I was left with the realization I was a single mom. My dream of having a happy Christian family, a white picket fence and dancing with Prince Charming at midnight was at the time shattered. He left me with no car and $500. Of course, he had the brand-new truck and $2,000 in tax return money driving off into the sunset.

I knew my nanny job making $400 a month would not suffice. Selfish jerk. With my family 1,500 miles away rent due of $550 and two young children. I had just been thrown into a sea of turbulence with sharks circling, or so it seemed.

Was this my moment of grace? In these defining moments you can choose to be a victim or a victor. This became the beginning of a self-discovering journey, full of mistakes, sins and lessons, the hard ones. I am here to tell you 20 years later that you CAN do it. But I hope you take a few moments to learn from me some advice I wish I had been given.

I am not sure if you know but each of us have six human needs. The need of certainty, uncertainty, significance, love/connection, growth and contribution. There are a few prominent teachers who I learned these from—Tony Robbins and Maslow. Everyone has all six human needs, yet two of them are more prominent than the others. They are usually based on what needs were not met when we were children. We go through life trying to find a way to have each of these needs met in a healthy or unhealthy way. Keep in mind your children need these met too.

I remember being at a football game that my son was playing in, when he was around 11. It was at a pivotal point in my life, I was in a relationship with an abusive man. Trying to find a way to break away from his sexual, physical and emotional abuse was occupying all my energy and attention. My son kept looking at me to see if I was watching him play. He was in the middle of the game and his focus should have been on who was trying to tackle him. It stuck in my memory as odd because at the time I did not **understand** how his needs were not being met. I knew they weren't, but did not understand what they were and how to meet them, let alone my own.

Sometimes my daughter would approach me when she just wanted some attention or to snuggle but I was busy. Busy cleaning the house, busy doing church activities, busy doing all of the tasks that piled up because I had to be the nurse, the accountant, the mechanic, the lawn care person, the shovel the snow person, therapist, taxi driver, the perfect Christian, the chef, etc. I would give everything I have to go back and just be *present* with her. To hold her, have a tea party or play with her. To not discipline her so strictly. My mind was always thinking of the next thing I had to do. All they needed was ME. All of me, my unconditional love and support. My unique independence, personality wisdom and full presence.

Please do not add anyone else into your circle until your six needs are being met for both you and your children in a healthy way. You may have been told you are Mom and Dad. That is wrong. You cannot be two people, so take a deep breath and relax. Just be you.

I have seen a lot of women try to be 'Dad' and confuse both their children and themselves. Contrary to popular belief Moms and Dads are different. There is a masculine and feminine energy. It is important to learn how to be authoritative and feminine. *A fine line I learned too late.*

When my children were young, I did not understand how to be authoritative. I treated them like they were my friends, and partner in the home. I would ask their input as if they were mature to help make major decisions. *I was too critical, judgmental and harsh at times.* I thought I was doing the right thing but realize now they just needed to be kids. Needed to be taught *why* I was making decisions so they could learn to be adults. You are not raising friends you are raising future adults. To have your kids meet all of your six needs is unhealthy.

Relationships, healthy vs. unhealthy. It took me a long time to work through the "I am enough" concept ... and I still am. My parents fought a lot when I was young. They did the best they could with what they had at the time... they were grieving and didn't know how to process it, taking it out on us. I did not understand it at the time, but it imprinted on me that I wasn't seen, or valued. A healthy relationship is one where you and the other person are individuals, and in the relationship share common interests that may overlap. A relationship free to be who God created you to be and loved unconditionally.

Through the many relationships I have had, I found myself at the age of 40 lost. 130 lbs. overweight, on my second marriage with someone who I did not respect. A moment of grace? I decided to start making healthy choices with what I ate, my entertainment, influences and relationships. It is important to find people who will support you through it all. Friends who will allow you to be you, not change you or not judge you. It is okay to need help. It does not mean you are failing, or not enough, or are doing anything wrong.

In cultures around the world families live in a community where family or friends pitch in. The US is one of the only places in the world where we are expected to do everything on our own – it is not normal. Be humble and accept help, but make sure it is with someone trustworthy.

Please, please, please do not put someone you've just dated for 6 weeks ahead of your children – or your Mom/Dad for that matter!! Moving in with them, having them make parental decisions or be a role model should only come after you have spent adequate time getting to know them. No matter how tempting it is to have someone carry the burden of finances and responsibilities take it slow – you will not regret it. My life would be so different now if I had. This goes for outside groups and activities too, Church, school, sports, music lessons etc.

How you spend your time is important. In 5 to 15 years your children will be adults. Right now, it may seem like an eternity, but I promise it will go fast. Prioritize your time. Take time for you. If you cannot take care of yourself how can you take care of your children? Read a book, play a game, go for a walk or meditate. You need time to be centered. If you feel like you just don't have time for this, start small, 5 minutes will go a long way for your mental health. *I wish I would have taken more time for this. As a result of not doing so I took my stress out on my children. Unless we break the cycle it will be handed down to each generation. Like it has mine.*

Set goals. I used to plan for a trip months in advance. Having something to look forward to got me through some of the most difficult days of my life. Quality time verses quantity time. Make time for fun! I used to feel guilty because I did not spend a lot of time with my children but, with all the mistakes I made I did do some things right. My daughter told me when my grandson was a few months old "Mom, I want you to make memories with him like you did us. You took us places and made memoires. Like looking for frogs. I want him to have that too."

When my children were young I found ways to do inexpensive things like hiking in the mountains of Wyoming and Colorado. Another thing I did was designated Friday nights as Family night. We would play games or watch a movie together.

Set boundaries, it is okay to say no to people or things. Be selective, have one extracurricular activity verses five. It used to be hard for me to tell people no. But I wish I could have seen the impact saying yes to everything had on my children. I know it is something you may not want to think about but how do you want your children to remember you when you die? The one person who stood by them, coached them, loved them unconditionally, laughed with them, made memories, was present with them. Or the person who put everyone and everything ahead of them? Who spent hours on social media. Life is a journey be patient with those you love, including yourself.

Forgiveness is a gift to the one who gives it. Forgive yourself, you are not perfect, but you are the only person who you'll be with every waking hour of every day. Be merciful to you. *Find your voice.*

Sara Olson
Empowerment Coach and Artist
My Courageous Masterpiece
United States of America
mycouageousmasterpiece.com

Finding My Brilliance through Forgiveness

by Debbie Belnavis-Brimble

"I would rather hold a grudge, fight, do anything, rather than forgive!" My inner child screamed with such conviction.

Forgiveness used to be such a dirty word to me many years ago, then I experienced its real magical powers. Whilst I was at University studying for my degree in computing and business, I was offered my very first job in information technology (IT) at the same University I had studied for years. I was so proud of myself; *I did it!* The greatest thing at the time was that it felt comfortable. For years, I had roamed the corridors of the very building I was going to be working in. It was familiar, and I loved familiarity. Don't you just love when everything falls into place, until it no longer feels right?

The years went by and I was promoted a few times, which

made me feel even more comfortable and content. Well, everyone in the organization had a job for life. Some had been there since they left high school and stayed until they retired. It wouldn't hurt to settle in. Little did I know, things were about to change. Don't get me wrong, I love change and it's inevitable; I accept that, however when we are living in a place of comfort, we fear any disruption to our lives. My disruption was a restructured department followed by a change in manager. The new manager had a different kind of leadership style—leading by *fear* and *favor*.

I observed her from a distance for years and noticed that if you followed her instructions to the letter; you had favor and if you didn't, you were left living in fear of her changing moods. I always operated from a very high standard for myself and everything I did, I delivered over and above. I was always trusted by managers in the past, because they valued my knowledge, experience and expertise. I was left to get on with the job at hand. It still astonishes me today that we don't always recognize and value the greatness in people when they are in our lives and when they leave, we want them to return. At that point I realized the value I had in my outgoing manager, a true leader.

At the time, I remember, my team and I were exceeding targets, actively involved in personal development and ensuring that the skills met the requirement for the department and organization, the team were supporting others around the department and making a significant impact within the organization. We were winning national awards for our processes, best-practices and leadership and gaining recognition for our combined efforts. I was involved in creating systems and processes to improve not only my teams' performances and objectives but also department-wide. I was proud of what I had created and how we worked together as a team. I loved seeing the team happy and excelling, especially in an environment where others were so visibly unhappy in their job.

The one thing that I noticed was that all the recognition was being redirected to my manager. I wasn't doing what I did for the glory of it, so if that's what she wanted, I would have been happy to pass it over to her. I did it to meet my own high standards, to fulfill my own needs of doing what I loved and pouring my all into it.

That would make a leader happy, right? Not in this case, I started to be micro-managed and if you have ever been micro-managed, you know how belittling it can make you feel. I could feel myself becoming overwhelmed by the unknown expectations, lack of appreciation and emotional strain. My confidence was decreasing and I could see myself withdrawing from others around me. After all, they allowed this to happen, didn't they?

I had always fought for the underdog and supported other colleagues through their challenges. Little did I know, I would become the underdog! When I looked around, there was no one to support me. Those I thought were my friends were fearful that they would be the next victim, and quickly disassociated themselves from me. It was times like these when you realize who your true friends are.

I couldn't understand why we couldn't work together as my previous manager, rather than being micro managed. There was no feedback to say that my work wasn't up to standard or that my performance wasn't meeting expectations.

Victim or Victress

I quickly sank into victim mode. I was always big in personal growth and development and noticed the signs in myself. How the hell could this have happened? Then it dawned on me, I was experiencing a passive form of bullying, although there was no physical pain, the impact is just as great and sometimes even worse.

I frequently heard my manager saying unkind things about me, my actions, and the way I worked to other colleagues, including other senior managers, yet saying only nice things to my face. The words I heard from her own lips were vicious sometimes and really drilled deep within, but what really hurt me most was knowing that some of my closest colleagues, who I considered as friends, said nothing and did nothing to defend me or support me.

I was so caught up by what she would say next, I could feel myself slowly losing sight of what was important to me. I felt isolated; I started to question myself, my ability, the way I worked and my own standards that supported me so well over the years. I knew that I did nothing wrong; I didn't say an unkind word about my bully, nor did I top performing in my job. I had nothing like this with my past manager; we had a mutual respect, great work ethics, high standards, and we were both qualified and experienced in our field. We had a great relationship; she spoke her truth and she gave invaluable feedback when needed. I wasn't used to working with someone who lead by fear. I decided that I had two options, fight or flight.

I had to fight; I was never a quitter. I complained to the Director about my manager and that changed things for a short period; I had a new manager for a few months. I noticed that things were slightly worse because my bully realized I wasn't going to sit back like everyone else she had victimized in the past. One thing bullies don't like and it's when you try to expose them and worse fight. It didn't stop me from going even higher and confiding in a senior manager within the organization who warned that I could make the complaint even more formal, however things would only get worse. When things like this happen, you have to reevaluate whether you are in the right environment. I have met so many women and men over the years that have shared their stories with me about what their work environments are like, and it really breaks my heart to know that this is such a common occurrence. When we think about bullying, we think about children being bullied in the playground. However, it is so real in the office place and sometimes it's by very senior managers who get away with it because they feel that they cannot be touched.

I knew that I had to do something, which supported me in making the next best decision of my life. I placed my stake in the ground by complaining. I fought for what I believed in. I stood up for myself and showed others that it is possible. I did what I was meant to do, now it was time to continue my journey in an environment that was more rewarding to my beautiful heart and soul. I wanted to have a greater impact in the world and support others in creating their waves, making our world a better place.

Before I left that organization, I started to regain my inner power. It takes it out of you when you are fighting for what you believe in. I fought for me and I was *proud*. Although there wasn't an outright winner from my experience, I would like to think that my actions have supported others who came after me in some way, by showing my bully that not everyone rolls over, some of us stand and fight. Even it if took everything out of me and even if I lost a few friends, who probably weren't true friends along the way, I was the outright winner. I left an environment that wasn't meant for me, it wasn't worthy of me. I know that it made other managers, including more senior managers, finally open their eyes for the first time in a long time. If you have had similar challenges in your life or career, know that there is nothing wrong with you, you may feel like a victim, remember, that's not your usual state and definitely not your permanent state. Reconnect with what is important to you and remain grounded always and know that you too have a choice. You don't have to allow others to determine your path.

It was hard to accept that I was vulnerable and fell into victim mode, yet I never gave up on myself. Even if my ripple was a small one, I am happy I chose to be the victress in my own way.

Invaluable Lessons

They say there is a lesson to learn in every experience and being bullied is no different. Looking around today, there is so much in the media about people taking their own life as a result of negative experiences like bullying. Imagine getting to the point where you feel so undervalued, worthless, isolated and trapped to take your own life.

I feel fortunate and blessed to not have gotten to the stage where I thought about ending my own life, but it could have easily happened. In my work as an Inner Brilliance Coach and Mentor, I have spoken to many clients who have had challenges in the workplace and been bullied by their peers, more senior and even more junior colleagues, and they have dealt with the challenge of taking their own life, then they sought support for themselves. If you have or are going through a similar situation, know that there is so much support available to you and tools that can support you in your healing journey.

Bullying in any form is wrong and although there is more focus about bullying in schools and online, workplace bullying[1], is increasing, isn't being discussed and it has a significant negative impact on the lives of so many.

I have learned to accept that how others perceive me, my actions and my behavior is their business and not mine. I decided that I couldn't change her behavior, her actions, or her response to me. I could however change my own response towards her.

Prior to this experience, I saw myself as a strong, independent, intelligent, inspirational and empowered woman filled with joy and love. The lesson I learned through this was that something was clearly misaligned within me. She didn't do anything to me; I allowed her to impact my life with her negative energy. I gave my power away for a while.

My Realization

When you are in a place where you are not fully aligned, it's easy to allow external factors to impact your you, no matter how resilient you usually are. Although I thought that everything was great in my life at the time, there was something clearly missing. I tried to fill the gap by throwing myself into work, supporting my team, ensuring that they had the resources to provide the excellent service, and enhancing my career by gaining numerous qualifications to be promoted. The gap wasn't closing. I was searching for external gratification from others and was working harder and harder to do a great job, to look good in their eyes.

I realized that the only person that could resolve this situation was me. I began working on myself. I reconnected with my values, my beliefs (including those that I used to limited myself). I got real intimate with myself as I went deeper and reconnected with my inner power. By this stage, I started using strategies that I knew about and some that I created and decided it was time for me to step into my brilliance by using my gifts for myself.

Through my own self work, I realized that the solution that was needed was forgiveness.

I want to make it crystal clear that forgiveness doesn't mean condoning unacceptable behavior. It doesn't mean forgetting the hurt you felt by someone's actions or their words, and it doesn't mean that you won't experience the hurt again, even from the same person. Forgiving someone means that you are making peace with what happened.

Releasing through Forgiveness

I observed through my work with clients, my research and my own personal experience that I see people holding onto things that happened 10, 20, 30+ years ago, which is impacting their lives in a negative way today.

I left that job feeling filled with negative emotions that were weighing me down, and I knew that I loved myself enough to let go, and release them to live the life I desired to the fullest. When you release the negative emotions and feelings with forgiveness, you open yourself up to raising your vibration to a more positive fulfilling one and bringing a significant amount of positive energy and abundance into your life.

Ho'oponopono Practice

I first heard about the Hawaiian Forgiveness Prayer Ho'oponopono when I trained as an Neuro Linguistics Programming (NLP) Practitioner and had to research it further. I learned that anything that I didn't want in my life is up to me to heal. The problem that I experienced was never a problem with others, it was with me and in order to change the person who caused me hurt, grief and pain, I had to change myself.

It's about total responsibly, total responsibility of my own reality, the good and the not so good. Healing using ho'oponopono means loving myself, and when I improved my life, I had to heal my life. So, healing the situation I was in and all other situations prior to that, all I had to do was heal myself through the power of forgiveness.

I believe in its power so much that I became a Certified Ho'oponopono Practitioner. It is also known as the forgiveness prayer or forgiveness ritual. Ho'oponopono means to make right and correct relationship problems.

For this practice, you repeat the following four phrases out loud or within your mind. The phrases are:
- I'm sorry
- Please forgive me
- Thank you
- I love you

Could forgiveness be this easy, I thought it would be yet another fad, I realized that this was a blessing from GUS (God, Universe, Source) in my healing journey.

Today, I love the woman I am, a wife, a mother, a daughter and granddaughter, a sister, a friend, a nurturer, a leader, a teacher, and a healer. A woman who demands her desires, knows her worth, knows that there are always infinite possibilities available to me, with a crystal clear vision of my future and has so much unconditional love for myself.

I used all the lessons I have learned and the strategies I have used in my own journey, and some that I crafted myself to support clients in their journey of healing through forgiveness and love. I'll go as far as to say, I'm a *locksmith*—providing the key to the door to unlock your brilliance. I giggle to myself every time I say that because my father really is a locksmith.

The critical aspects of forgiveness are always:
- Practice forgiveness from the heart, in its purest form.
- Forgive unconditionally, with no limitations.
- This is a journey, not a race, so forgiveness is a daily practice.

When you learn to forgive yourself, you give yourself the power to move away from the past and into the present, giving you control of your life again. What are some of the things that you are holding onto that you are ready to forgive yourself for?

Your Steps to Forgiveness

My mission is to inspire, teach and guide women globally to identify, accept, embrace, nurture and love who she truly is and forgiveness is part of that process. Show yourself some love by forgiving yourself first. Forgive yourself for:
- Not always believing in yourself.
- Not giving yourself permission to shine bright.
- Not loving yourself unconditionally until now.

- Giving your power away.
- Not fully owning who you truly are.

Forgiveness is such a critical aspect in the healing process that I have created a program to support clients through healing, through forgiveness. I have worked with clients who are on their healing journey, healing their wounds from childhood trauma, sexual abuse, self-harming, abandonment, fear, shame and so much more. I created the *Forgive and be Free Program,* supporting you in stepping into freeing yourself from your anger and resentment, allowing you to soar even higher.

This program is available through the Inner Brilliance Academy at www.innerbrillianceacademy.com.

Debbie Belnavis-Brimble
Inner Brilliance Coach & Mentor, #1 International Best-Selling Author, Publisher
Behind those Heels, Carnelian Moon Publishing
United States of America & United Kingdom
behindthoseheels.com, innerbrillianceacademy & carnelianmoonapublishing.com

Releasing the Control of Food and My Secret Shames

by Jennifer Hernandez

I have been on a weight loss journey for over 20 years of my life. Actually, over 30 going all the way back to middle school.

I feel like where I am now is out of hiding. I was hiding. Inspired by my sister, my favorite athlete, I challenged myself and started to step up. Unhealthy at first and then finding where I feel I am today, living my calling. Sharing my truth and feeling amazing, and putting light on those shames and secrets I used to hold in my dieting.

As I share my story of home and overcoming, this is my reminder to you that no matter how many times you think you fail, you truly are not defined by your past, unless you stop and stay there. I have learned over and over that, the things you are attempting to do — lose weight, grow your business, or find your ideal partner — those things that you can't seem to achieve is not that you aren't meant to have them or achieve them. You repeatedly get to the same "wall" again and again because you haven't become the person that achieves or has those things yet. You simply need to learn and become the person who gets there.

Let me take you back to a few of my previous selves.

Looking back, my health and my love life have always been deeply entwined. I can remember being in middle school, taking quarters from the change table in the hallway. I would sneak out after school to CVS to buy a big family size of BBQ chips and finishing the entire bag while watching after-school specials. Remember those 80s babies? I always felt they were talking right to me. By the time the chip bag was empty the main character had their life together and somehow, I was sitting there thinking I was a mess, fat, and ugly. I would look at the empty chip bag and realize I had to do something. I had to get rid of the proof. So, I would crumple the bag up, wrap it in paper towels, and then dig down to the bottom of the garbage can and hide it there. If no one knows no harm, right? Chips don't matter. That is what I thought. But there was harm, and someone did know. I knew, and I knew it was wrong, but I did it anyway.

This continued through middle school and was probably one of the reasons I started getting heavy. I don't remember my exact size, but I was bigger than any of my friends and my belly was the same as my growing chest. I rocked a pixie cut and made myself cool by putting a Z line in the one side and slicking over with LA Gear Gel. I remember these things because I wanted to fit in and hide how uncomfortable I was in my body with trendy things. Like that time, I managed to talk my mom into letting me get a spiral perm. It didn't work though. Everyone saw and knew.

One very painful time on the local bus home, an 8th grade boy made a big loud deal to point it out. He brushed my folded arms away from me and said something like, "Are you a boy or a girl? I can't tell if you are just super fat or that you maybe have boobs." As sensitive and loving as I am, I honestly can't tell you how I managed to stay silent and not cry in that moment. I felt like a wall was inside of me. I just sat frozen and wished the bus would get to the 13th street exit fast.

It was shortly after that I secretly started my first diet. Well, I can't really call it a diet, as I would just skip as many meals as I could. I would tie off sweatshirts around my waist to sleep trying to compress my belly flat. When I was at my dad's house, I would close the door and do the Nordic Track cross skier in front of a mirror, using my nighttime sweatshirt trick to help the sweat. No one knew what I was doing. I hid it all well. The thing you might find crazy, I wouldn't go back and change it. Although this unhealthy relationship with food and my body turned into a repetitive cycle through high school.

During my 8th grade, I faced many challenges and I started leaning out from my tactics, or maybe because I was growing and my body was changing too. I started gaining attention from boys and even had my first love. As long as I had someone actively loving me, I would be fine I thought. Two relationships later, I was a senior in high school. My boyfriend encouraged me to play field hockey which I fell in *love* with, then on to cross country and basketball. Being active for more than an hour a day year-round really trimmed me out. I look back at my pictures and can't believe I still felt like that round 6th and 7th grader, because I loved what I saw in my high school pictures.

Our minds believe what we tell it, and I told myself I was a big boned girl. When my boyfriend of 3 years went to college a year ahead of me and I visited him, I found myself going back to my middle school tricks. I compared myself to the more fit and petite women and would sneak Dextrum and the Hollywood juice diet on weekends. He almost caught me once and it was almost a time I could have confessed and addressed the harm I was doing to my body. I remember the struggle in the kitchen. I dropped a pill and he tried to grab it before I did so he could see what I was taking. I wouldn't tell him because I was embarrassed that I had a urinary tract infection and was taking AZO. He later compared the pill and found out that it really was for a UTI, and I got away with it, that time. The things he didn't see but must have suspected.

My 20s, and my early 30s, it is facing this struggle over and over that made me who I am today. I am able to give back and inspire, or speak to someone struggling because I know how it feels and I can say, I have overcome. I have learned and clearly see that our biggest struggles are actually the gift we are meant to give and share to this world. And we must be willing to face them, conquer them, and share how we did so.

Looking back, I see that the changes in my relationships would lead to secret eating, pill taking, patches, wraps, and any weight loss tactics that I could use to fix my body. I didn't see my body shape as a result of my eating or emotions, I saw it like a puzzle or project that just had to be pushed, scraped, or manipulated so that it could be loved. In my mind, my body was the reason I wasn't getting love, or it would be the reason my relationship would end, because I didn't look good enough. I didn't see the value in myself.

In my 20s, I was working in an office and exposed to take out and breakroom donuts for the first time. Having been active in high school sports, the weight started to jump on. My motto through to early 30s was *'free food is good food.'* I would sit at my desk and have iceberg lettuce and hotdogs (no bun because, Atkins was popular). Then, I would leave work and get drive-thru before working my second job at the mall. Eventually, I was too hungry and the donuts looked too good and I would eat three or four before lunch. Whenever anyone was ordering out, I was *in* and I would eat kid's meals on the way home. Then, stop at the gas station three blocks from my house to throw away the drive-thru proof. The little girl in me, hiding chip bags in wadded up paper towels in the bottom of the garbage can never went away.

Most of my 20s was like this. You would get a different sized me every six months, which was quite dramatic. I would go from wearing a size 14 to needing to buy 24s for the wedding or family gathering overnight. My weight started to impact my health. I have paid thousands in insurance copays with the visits for heartburn, migraines, and kidney stones, diverticulitis flare ups and antibiotics for monthly bouts of cold. I never saw my health and body being connected to my mind and emotional health. I still looked at my body as given to me big. I saw my body as an issue I was given. I was born big boned. I was meant to always be big. I just had to fix it from the outside or hide it.

And fixing it took external tools and shaping, not internal. When I was 28, I was working two part time jobs, one as a bank teller and the other a candle party business. One day at my bank teller job, I was pistol whipped during a bank robbery, a life altering moment. The counseling and therapy I received lead to my husband and I choosing divorce. This changed the direction of my life.

I fell in love, or infatuation with a man at work who made the 300 plus pound me feel seen and loved. I fell hard and followed him out of the area, disconnecting from my family and friends. It was a fairy tale fantasy life. The signs were there which I didn't see or ignored because I had my love goggles on, as he referred to it. I refused to see the legal issues that we faced, and eventually the fact that we were just not compatible anymore. The best parts of those years was my son, who was created in absolute love. Whether I was truly loved back doesn't matter, at least my son will always know that he was wanted by me and I was in love when I made him.

I became a single mom, working long hours, having no child support, government assistance, or contributions. I did whatever I had to at work to make sure all the bills were paid. When I wasn't working, I was a zombie. I would pick Joseph up and then retreat to my small single room rental home in Bath and play on the floor with him while watching TV. I would often order out or buy food on the way home, and then after he would fall asleep, I would watch Law and Order until 2 a.m. I still didn't like my body, but after paying for daycare, the gym wasn't possible. Looking back, I really didn't want to lose weight. I was still in love with his father, although there was no way that would work, so I decided to be alone forever. At least until Joseph was out of high school, then I would be allowed to *start my life*.

I realized now, that I used food and unhealthy eating to fill emotional voids. I would eat because food was *touching me* when there was no one around to hug or be with me. I would eat food when I was happy because I wanted to hug — I'm a hugger and physical touch is my primary love language. I didn't know this then. I just knew it seemed like getting appetizers, dinner, and dessert would fix everything. Yet nothing changed, I just got sadder and more uncomfortable.

This was the beginning of my renaissance period. I spent a lot of nights crying on my living room floor or biting my pillows in tears before going to sleep. I was hurting and struggling but I didn't want anyone to know. Thankfully my sister was starting her journey as a triathlete and Joey and I went and watched her. I remember that race clearly, it was another moment that changed the course of my life. Seeing my sister conquer this crazy thing called a triathlon at Steelman opened my eyes. I saw my sister, a full-time paramedic on night shifts and single mom of a tween at the time, conquer and do crazy hard things. I knew there was sacrifice and work put in to achieve what she did. She showed me there is always a way — you just have to start. I saw other men and women twice my size get out of the water and jump on their bikes and go. I was amazed. It never came to my mind to think about doing a sport. I mean, wasn't sports only an option for students and professionals?

My sister is my favorite athlete and this day started the chain reaction of what is my most amazing and wonderful life. Watching her and being at the event, I found the Lehigh Valley

Road Runners free 5k and decided to give running another try. This would be my first time since high school. I can't tell you why but I also started emailing myself after that race — no one told me to. I didn't read it anywhere. I was inspired by a different life and what mine could be like. I emailed myself about the loving and strong mother I was. I told myself that I would light up the room when I walked in. That I had a faithful man who loved me and raised Joseph as his own. I wrote about owning a house and who I would be.

I started going to the group runs and fast forward to running into my husband. This man who truly loves me. Is the most amazing and only father Joseph has ever known. And who truly loves Joseph as his own. I am living what I wrote to myself in all those emails.

I got down to 246 pounds, and I looked great — my lowest weight in years, from over 300 pounds, the second time in my adult life. I was eating a little better after making some vegan friends in the running groups who shared food ideas, and me avoiding fast food. I was running almost 7 days a week, while pushing a jogging stroller. I also was being my middle school self, secretly taking fat loss pills, wrapping myself in saran wraps, and tight shirts, and sweatshirts at night as well as some pretty drastic juice cleanses.

There was so much good that came from my first years running and then with my husband. So why did I gain 70 pounds? I was in an amazing, loving relationship, owned my home, and living my positive life with my run group and health friends. I felt like I failed. I was convinced that something was medically wrong. I was juicing, we were 100% vegan, I was running and doing hour long boot camps for obstacle course races. But things started to change in late 2015 — I got married, my new husband moved in that same week, and I had to stop my secret pills, patches and wraps. I hid them for a while and tried to use them in my *closet* room, but when you live with someone and share everything it's hard to hide. So, I stopped my weight loss tricks.

As I settled into my new marriage and new job, I ended up working long hours and staying late at the office, missing the run groups. Now that the running and the quick fixes were out, I was eating vegetables, juicing and eating all the free food. My 20s motto of *'Free food = good food'* was still going strong. I wouldn't be surprised if I consumed as much as two of my coworkers or more combined. I've been secret eating and hiding wrappers since I was 12 — I was a *pro*.

What I hadn't learned yet is that my food, mindset, and body were connected. I made a doctor's appointment in July 2016, after gaining 70 pounds in less than a year. I was sure there was something to be fixed that they could prescribe or cut out what was causing this issue. A few thousand dollars later — internal and external exams, scans, and bloodwork. Thankfully, I wasn't even prediabetic and I wasn't even thankful. I was crushed.

This was the low point I needed to put those last pieces together. I had a real hard cry that night. Alone, hiding from my son and husband, remembering the fight with my husband earlier. It was about my 2 hours of hitting the snooze button every morning that disturbed him, and if I didn't change it we would need to sleep in separate rooms. I thought about how tired I was after work with barley any energy or time to give Joey any of his mom. I would cover up my body and pull away and glare at my husband if he tried to touch me. The man who truly loved me and sees me for me no matter what size I was, and I was pushing him away.

So I did what you do to find a solution. I was looking for a distraction to numb the feelings by surfing Netflix and Facebook and yes, the start to my solution was found. I saw a post offering a 7-day mason jar salad group and I honestly looked at it, rolled my eyes, and said, "What could a salad hurt?" I messaged the woman and after still saying no for a few weeks I felt ready. Then I panicked and all my past failures started whispering at me—this would be another waste of money like all those quick fixes you did. And I started backing away. Thank goodness she kept checking in on me and inviting me because that gave me just enough belief that I could borrow and say yes.

Thankfully, I said yes to that coach and the company she represented, which was a well known brand that supports people around the world in connecting them to nutritional tools and workouts. It gave me a total body and mind solution and now I am an independent coach with the company and a certified mindset mentor and help people in the United States, Canada, France and the United Kingdom.

It was the keys I was missing. It wasn't immediate big weight loss but I set myself up for success by committing to be here in a year and surrounding myself with a community that was working on their mindset, and learning that pulled me forward. I was down almost 80 pounds in my first year of portioned eating, drinking my vitamin shake (not a weight loss suppressant shake, it's just how I chose to take my vitamins now), working out 20 to 30 minutes a day, and reading books while sharing and leaning with others doing the same.

In my second year, the company released a mindset nutrition course and *this* was it for me. For the first time in my life I no longer was scared of regaining the weight, and food no longer controlled me. If I wanted pizza I could have it without shame. I released that *"free food = good food"* motto and actually enjoyed eating my packed lunch, even during free meals at work. I felt better, and I now had a healthier mindset, understanding of emotional connection with food. Plus the work I did on myself to understand that my *whole* body is me — my mind, heart, health, weight, and shape. It's all me.

I am not at my ideal fitness level yet. I have loose skin, stretch marks and sometimes, the skin under my arm wiggles more than others from evicting 120 pounds, which I have kept off for 3 years. I love it all, because through this journey, I found my voice, and I'm sharing my gift to the world, giving hope. Because of my personal results, I was feeling great, and love my business. I got certified in our mindset courses and now coach others on their journey — doing it all together.

There were a lot of me's. I love them all. They all pushed through different struggles that I learned from and created the me I am today, even if I learned some of the lessons repeatedly.

If I could reach out to one of my old me's when she was in the cycle what would I do?

If I could go back to that middle school girl stealing quarters and hiding chip bags?

If I could go to that high school girl taking water pills, Stacker 2 and Dexatrim?

If I could go back to that single mother crying on the floor?

If I could go back to that 20 and 30 something drive-thru aficionado?

If I could talk to that runner finding herself and love but relying on quick fixes.

If.

I can't go back to those versions of me but I can reach someone secretly struggling in those moments now, you are not alone. I know someone needs my story because I needed someone else's story to spark my inspiration and belief. You are not bad, broken or wrong. You don't need a whole new you to be loved. All you need is to make the decision that this doesn't serve you.

I prolonged my pain longer than I had to and repeated the cycles for over 25 years because I was scared to reach out and ask for help. I felt like I was less than to have a plan and a coach.

If I could go back in time, I would hug myself so tight and tell her I love her and she is SO strong. I would tell her it is not weak to ask for help, it is actually one of the bravest things you can do. I would tell her, *"You don't need to wake up and be perfect, you don't need a whole new you. You just need to take that first step and keep going."*

It is the start that stops most people. I can't guarantee how quickly you will get results, that depends on your willingness to use the tools and work with me or the coach you chose.

Love yourself today as you are and celebrate her for being brave enough to start over again and again and keep learning and going forward. Change is hard, but it is also so beautiful.

Ask yourself:

Is this my limit?

Is this my best life?

Is this the best I will ever be or is this where I grow?

I will choose growth every time and I invite you to grow with me. Progress is the best feeling you will ever have. I know how it is, I know it isn't easy, and yet I know it is so worth it.

You can do this. Yes, you can!

Jennifer Hernandez
Mindset Nutrition Coach
2 Be Happy and Healthy
2behappyandhealthy.com
United State of America

Jennifer Hernandez

Your Message Inspires the World

Now, more than ever, the voice of women need to be heard, valued and shared. As women, we are the nurturers of the world. We spend our lives supporting everyone around us, caring for, uplifting, teaching.

As you read the stories, think about how they connected with you, what were your thoughts as you read? How did the stories make you feel? Do you see yourself in the stories? Do you feel inspired to take action in your own life? How can you share your story in the world to inspire others?

We know here at *Behind those Heels* that everyone has a story, because you have been on your own unique journey. Often we think that our stories are not as impactful or powerful as others, yet, someone is waiting to hear from you. Someone could be waiting to hear about your story to support them in whatever way they need it to at this exact moment in time. We have all shared our stories to inspire others around the world to take action, move foward in embracing your dreams, embrace who you are truly meant to be, love yourself unconditionally, forgive like your life depends on it, place yourself first always, when your own cup is filled to the brim and overflowing, you can feed others from your overflow. We are all fuller for sharing our journey with you, and although we are all still on our healing journey, we continue to heal, we continue to grow, we continue to learn and we will continue to share our truth.

We would love for you to join our movement and share your message if you are called to, or if you know somoene who would be perfect for this opportunity. Join the Behind those Heels movement by visiting our website below and sharing your story either on our podcast or in one of our future books. We love meeting new members and as we continue to grow, we continue to share even more.

All that we do, we do to support you, your loved ones, your family, friends, community and ultimately the world. How can you make a contribution and create your ripple in the world. We challenge you to share your story today and support us in making an even greater ripple around the world, one drop at a time. We know that behind those heels, everyone has a story to share!

Warmest blessings to you always, keep inspiring!

About Behind those Heels

The concept of B*Behind those Heels* is the vision of Cassie Ferrer who met a group of well-dressed, accomplished, and confident women from her volunteer network. These women shared unexpected stories on how they overcame their challenges and found fulfillment in lives. Cassie was instantly inspired by their uplifting stories. In talking to these remarkable women, Cassie realized that behind those heels, every woman has a story and she made it her personal vision to share these stories to inspire women around the world.

Teaming up with Debbie Belnavis-Brimble, Inner Brilliance Coach and Mentor to women, #1 International Best-Selling Author and publisher, who shares a similar passion, and currently supports women in sharing their message through her publishing brand Carnelian Moon Publishing. This led to the birth of the movement that is Behind those Heels.

Our Purpose
To create a movement of women sharing their powerful stories using various platforms including podcast, books and events, encouraging others to take action and seek support to enhance their lives.

Our Vision

To inspire and empower millions of women worldwide by sharing powerful stories of extraordinary women through multiple platforms.

Our Mission

Inspiring women around the globe to seek fulfillment and living with purpose by sharing powerful stories and messages of remarkable women who have led extraordinary lives.

We document the journeys of women and share their stories through multiple platforms, including books, podcasts, events and so much more. The goal to bring out these stories is to provide hope and possibilities, to inspire, and empower others to make bold decisions about their own lives then take massive steps to enhance their lives in positive ways.

Jennifer Hernandez

About Our Authors

Adele Mason
WomenShift Coaching, Inc.
Canada

Adele Mason has a BA and MA in Sociology and received her certification as a life coach in August 2019. She founded WomenShift Coaching in July 2019, in order to wage peace in the war on people with substance use disorders through education, information, conversation, and above all else, love.

Adele is a recovering alcoholic and, in memory of the battle she found and almost lost with alcohol, now walks alongside others as they seek to heal towards a sober life and healthy, effective living.

Connect with Adele:
Website: womenshiftcoaching.com

Cassie Ferrer
Behind those Heels & Numbers Nerd Consulting
United States of America

Cassie is an Award-Winning financial leader who has worked in the financial industry for 15 years. She is an author, host of *Behind those Heels Podcast*, and Founder of *Behind those Heels* and *Numbers Nerd Consulting, LLC*.

After working for two top financial institutions, Cassie started to look deeper within and questioned her purpose which led to the launch of *Behind those Heels*. While meeting all the amazing business owners through the podcast, she realized how she could use her expertise, her MBA, and degrees in finance and marketing to support business owners to improve financial health and increase business cash flow.

Cassie resides in Florida with her family and enjoys going to Disney theme parks. She enjoys reading company's annual reports, listening to personal development audiobooks, and practicing yoga.

Connect with Cassie:
Website (Share Your Message): behindthoseheels.com
Website (Wealth Coach): numbersnerdconsulting.com

Ruth Murray
Seeds of Change Mindset Coaching
New Zealand

Ruth lives in New Zealand and coaches mainly women who are in recovery from a narcissistic relationship. She runs two monthly courses for this express purpose. She also does one on one coaching, it is really dependent on each woman and what suits her best. Ruth is a Mental Health Nurse by profession, although she hasn't practiced for many years.

She is passionate about helping women to live a life of purpose and direction and helping them to regain their worth and value. Her own experiences support her in knowing that without this we continue to repeat the pattern of getting stuck in narcissistic relationships.

As a single mother of six gorgeous adult children, and three grandchildren, she loves spending time with them and they have her heart.

Connect with Ruth:
Facebook: facebook.com/ruth.murray.7737
YouTube: youtube.com/channel/UCvEmxG-k3FjZRJLfhXyJFlg

Georgia Pomrenke
VP of Human Resources at SIRS, Inc.
United States of America

Georgia Pomrenke is the VP of Human Resources of SIRS, Inc. in Southern Indiana. She is also an author that goes by the name of Georgia Marie. Georgia is married to an amazing RN and is the fur-momma of soon to be two fur babies. As part of her side-hustle and a means for healing, Georgia is a blogger who shares her journey to improve emotional health through stories. Find out more about Georgia, her work, and her blog supporting others in their healing.

Connect with Georgia:
Website: GeorgiaMarie3333.com
Instagram: @georgiamarie3333

Michelle Montero
Marketing Strategist at Michelle Montero
United States of America

Michelle is a young entrepreneur, who is a spiritually guided, creative, who loves nature and animals. She is a web design and digital marketing expert and studied graphic design at high school, practiced it hands-on during her spare time, and realized it is something she really enjoyed and fell in love with. She has perfected the art and now helps business and mindset coaches tackle behind-the-scenes tasks so they can live a fulfilling, productive and, stress-free life while scaling a thriving online business.

Connect with Michelle:
Website: michellemontero.us

Debbie Brady
Ending Stigma Together, LLC
United States of America

Debbie has over 20 years of experience in the mental health field in both the inpatient and community settings, including schools, homeless shelters, and as an advocate.

As a result of her own personal experience of living with long-term depression since childhood, and also battling anorexia in college, she has developed techniques that have not only helped her personally and countless others. In addition to her personal and professional experience, she holds an undergraduate degree in Psychology and a Master's Degree in Counseling. She is the author of the Amazon #1 Best-Selling book *Depression Survival Guide: Your Path To A Joy-Filled Life* released in 2019.

She currently lives in Florida with her husband, 4 sons, 3 dogs, and their cat. She is a proud Philadelphia native and says it was the best decision for her mental health to move south.

Connect with Debbie:
Website: endingstigmatogether.com

Tania Hunter-Gilligan
Ignite Your Soul
New Zealand

Tania is a Dream Creator, entrepreneur, and author, inspiring women to love their inner Goddess, to grow, choose to live in their full potential and shine like they were born to.

Her greatest desire is to make a positive impact on the world, to leave a small footprint, a big difference in the lives of people, animals, and our planet, and a legacy for her children, grandchildren, and the generations to follow.

She understands this starts from the heart of humans, women in particular. Women are naturally nurturing and have a strong and heart-driven desire to give for the betterment of our world.

Tania is married to the love of her life, her equal, her rock, and her best friend. She is the mum of four children and two stepchildren, all adults and unique and beautiful souls in their own right.

Connect with Tania:
Facebook: facebook.com/igniteyoursoulonfire

Sara Olson
My Courageous Masterpiece
United States of America

Sara is an Empowerment Coach, author, and artist with 20 years of leadership experience. Sara has been featured in Forbes Magazine representing a previous company she worked for.

She is a courageous, adventurous, generous leader who enjoys the little things in life. So many of her characteristics, including her quirky sense of humor, can be attributed to her parents, God rest their souls.

It is Sara's goal to utilize her books, art, and businesses to establish a Non-profit organization for Single Parents. Sara is currently writing a book about her own story which shares her journey as a single parent. She believes that things happen for us, not to us, we are never too old, young, fat, skinny, or (whatever excuse to fill in the blank) to make a difference in your family, community, and ultimately the world and to rewrite your story to have that "Happy Ending" and make your dreams of reality.

Connect with Sara:
Website: mycouageousmasterpiece.com

Debbie Belnavis-Brimble
Inner Brilliance Academy, Behind those Heels, Carnelian Moon Publishing
United States of America & United Kingdom

Debbie has been in the personal growth industry for over 12 years as the Inner Brilliance Coach and Mentor. She is the Founder of the *Inner Brilliance Academy* and Co-Founder of *Carnelian Moon Publishing* and *Behind those Heels*. She is also a #1 International Best-Selling Author of several books.

She is a life-long learner who loves quenching her thirst for knowledge and holds multiple degrees in Business, Coaching and Mentoring qualifications, a Master Neuro-Linguistics Programming (NLP) Practitioner, Neuro-Linguistics Programming (NLP) Coach, Time Line Therapy Practitioner, Hypnotherapy Practitioner and even trained in Performance Improvements for Neurodiverse Conditions.

Connect with Debbie:
Website (Coaching & Mentoring): innerbrillianceacademy.com
Website (Publishing): carnelianmoonpublishing.com
Website (Share Your Message): behindthoseheels.com

Jennifer Hernandez
2 Be Happy and Healthy
United State of America

Jennifer is a busy mother of a 9 year old boy and wife. She found her passion helping others with their health after living a 20 year cycle of losing and gaining weight to over 300 lbs more than 3 times. She has turned her past failures and feeling worthless into a gift for helping others.

This is her first appearance as an author. She often speaks to small groups sharing her story, inspiration, and tips to start the health journey. Her mission is to inspire, empower, & support families to be their happiest and healthiest and she offers comprehensive family solutions for both fitness and food.

Jennifer's favorite words of encouragement are *"Yes you can, I know it is hard, I know you can do it."* Her hope is to inspire others to action and ask themselves *"is this my limit or is this where I grow?"* If you are ready to grow and live your best life and start your own journey she is just a message away!

Connect with Jennifer:
Website: 2behappyandhealthy.com
Facebook: facebook.com/Jensbean33

Behind those Heels

www.ingramcontent.com/pod-product-compliance
Lightning Source LLC
Chambersburg PA
CBHW072203100526
44589CB00015B/2345